ONE WEEK IN LA | TWO YEARS LATER

ONE WEEK IN LA

TWO YEARS LATER

KODY CHRISTIANSEN

Official Book Website
www.HeartbreakDreams.com

Twitter/Instagram
KodyKitty

Facebook
www.Facebook.com/HollywoodHeartbreakNewYorkDreams

Email
info@heartbreakdreams.com

Copyright © 2017 by Kody Christiansen

All rights reserved. No part of this publication may be reproduced, distributed, or transmitted in any form or by any means, including photocopying, recording, or other electronic or mechanical methods, without the prior written permission of the author, except in the case of brief quotations embodied in critical reviews and certain other noncommercial uses permitted by copyright law.

All photos are from the author's personal collection.

First Edition

978-1-946022-09-7

To all those who seek redemption.

The first step is to forgive yourself for who you were before. Then, face your fears and go bravely into your new world with clarity and light. Ask forgiveness from others, but be ready if it takes them time to see the change.

Things will get better every day, if you continue to stay strong and remember to always dream big.

FOREWORD

In my foreword to Kody Christiansen's first book, *Hollywood Heartbreak/New York Dreams*, I ended it with the prophetic words, "his life is still a work in progress." Little did I realize how much life Kody could live in a single week in Los Angeles.

Kody came back to the City of Angels for a book signing. He told me of both his fears and hopes of returning to the scene of the crime. The crime being the dismantling of his life in the shadows of the Hollywood sign. Those who've read his first book know the torturous journey he took here. Drug and alcohol abuse being just the tip of a horribly destructive iceberg.

The Kody who arrived in Los Angeles looked years younger and, most importantly, generated extreme happiness. The demons still fought to conquer this renewed optimism, but he seemed to be winning the battle. What gave me hope was seeing the effusive exuberance that reminded me of the twenty-two year old I had met eleven years earlier. He was both brash and incorrigible when he walked into my business, but he knew what he wanted and how to get it. These traits would serve him well during the week he worked his magic in La La Land.

The spotlight seems to follow this charismatic wanderer. He attracts joy and chaos wherever he goes. He's like that proverbial moth drawn to the light, but always wary of the deadly heat of getting too close. Life is never mundane in his world, making his stories that much more compelling. This is a book about making dreams come true, while also remembering, heartbreak can be just around the corner.

Thomas Rosa
Cake and Art
West Hollywood, California

CONTENTS

11	Prologue: One Week in LA
17	Wednesday. Day One
37	Thursday. Day Two
61	Friday. Day Three. The Big Day
77	Saturday. Day Four
97	Sunday. Day Five
109	Monday. Day Six
121	Tuesday. Day Seven
133	Wednesday. Day Eight. Full Circle.
153	Thursday. Day Nine
163	Epilogue: One Week in NY
175	Photo Gallery
197	Acknowledgements
203	Resources for Hope and Help
207	Famous Last Words

PROLOGUE: ONE WEEK IN LA

EIGHT MONTHS after the story of *Hollywood Heartbreak/New York Dreams*, I found myself with the opportunity to face my fears and finally return to Los Angeles where I had been invited to hold a book signing at Book Soup, the world-renowned book shop on Sunset Boulevard.

The city where I had met my ultimate heartbreaker. The place where I wallowed in the pit of destructive drug addiction and alcoholic despair. The smallest big city I have ever lived in, where I first tasted betrayal and a hint of homelessness. The city, my "home," where I contemplated suicide over a cup of coffee and a line of Splenda looking like cocaine, sitting on a table at a famous 24-hour diner, before being handcuffed and nearly arrested. The glitziest city in the world that had turned me into the darkest and dimmest version of myself. The city I had to run away from.

"Face your fears," the proverbial THEY always say. Easy enough to say for a faceless entity, but not as easy to do for the actual person who had to take on the task. Who were THEY anyway? Were THEY going to be by my side when I boarded a plane again for the first time in over two years? Were THEY going to hold my hand when I landed in Hollywood and dared to walk back into the places where I had completely lost myself so many times? Were THEY going to give me advice on what to do when I saw the man who broke my heart but ultimately became the catalyst that forced me onto the beautiful path my life had taken?

No. It was I, and I alone, who had to fight this battle. I was in such a better place in my life at this point anyway. My book had been out for almost 3 months, had already received rave reviews, and had been a number one seller on many lists. I had made a complete 180 degree turn as a human being, and I was now inspiring others to find their own divine paths. I was even inspiring some of the people I used to hang out with when I was such a wreck of a person. The truest example of "if he can do it, I can do it!"

Facing those people was a fear weighing on my chest, as well -- facing these people, my "friends," who seemed to turn their backs on me at my most desperate and lowest point in my life. How would they react to the new me? Would I even want them in my life anymore? Could the important people in my LA life embrace my change and accept my apologies for the life I lived? For the pain and anguish I caused them? Would I be the one to help them now? To save them from the edge of their own darkest days?

As I packed my suitcase for my return to Hollywood, I had flashbacks of how I got to where I was at that very moment: the drunken haze and homeless shelters that were the backdrop for my first year and a half in New York City; the evangelical who was on late night TV the evening that I decided to quit drinking and using drugs for good; the friends I had made in the shelters who became like family to me. Flashes of my time as a recurring character on NBC's "The Blacklist," when I became a Screen Actors Guild member and the time I hosted my own sold-out Off Broadway show as my alter ego, Sarah Summers. The weekend that Tim came to New York and met Clarke, Catherine, and all my new family of friends at my book release event at The Stonewall Inn National Monument. Every amazing memory rushed through my head.

As I zipped the last pocket full of my new big city wardrobe, I had a feeling that this trip just might be a mind-opening journey, one I had to take to continue to grow and move forward as a human being. Would the voice of darkness and old temptations be stronger than the new-found words of hope and light that now constantly surrounded my train of thought? Before I left, I consulted with my "spiritually adoptive parents" for advice.

Tim, the owner of the cake shop in Hollywood, who had become like a father to me over the years, was excited for this next step in my sober series of adventures. He helped me get a plane ticket with his Virgin America connection. He was still always there for me, with a little monetary help (but now very infrequently), as I started to make a good living with my acting work and my server job.

Things at Parigot, the French restaurant, were still going well, too. I stopped by the night before I left for my trip to consult with my "French Momma," Catherine. She and I had connected years ago over spiritual conversations, glasses of wine (back when I was drinking), and, eventually, over her motherly attitude towards me that helped push me into the person I had become today.

Like mother, like surrogate son, she had an alter ego as well: "Lady Catherine." This name was created out of her very serious love and wisdom of tarot cards. "Lady Catherine" would give readings to customers for $25 plus a free glass of wine, but for her spiritually adoptive son at another turning point in his life, it was free.

When we sat down at the marble four-seater table situated halfway inside the restaurant and halfway out onto the downtown SoHo street, I could feel the energy all around us. I hadn't asked her for a reading in a long time, maybe in over a year, because I wholeheartedly believed in its power and was afraid of what the cards might say.

Sipping my hot peppermint tea from the white diner-style coffee mug, I watched as she began to shuffle the worn deck of ornately designed tarot cards. Looking across the table with eyes almost the same bright color blue as mine, she asked, "Are you ready to see what the cards have to say, Kaleb?"

There was no going back now. "Yes," I said confidently, as she handed me the deck to cut. When the piles were separated and my cards were chosen, she began to decipher the messages that appeared to her. Hers eyes lit up when she saw The Star card, and she frowned when she flipped The Devil card. She turned the rest of the cards over and let me in on their secret meanings.

"This trip will be absolute magic for you! I see mostly all good things in the cards here. You are really going to benefit from this trip. Spiritually and emotionally," she spoke in her comforting French accent, as she took a sip of Merlot in her fancy wine glass.

Putting the glass down in front of her, she continued, "But beware. There is temptation all around you. And you will see him again. It's up to you to decide how you will handle all this. But I know you will make the right decisions. You've come too far to go backwards now."

The "him" she was referring to was most definitely the rock star who had made me love again and then ripped my heart out of my chest at my weakest moment. A real gem of a man. I hadn't heard anything from him since I left Los Angeles over 2 years prior, but I had heard things about him. He was arrested multiple times, lost his beautiful house where we once spent some magical moments, and was still drinking and using drugs daily. I guess some things never change.

It was so strange for me to think that some of

the people I left behind in LA were still living the same lives when my own life had changed so dramatically. Was I really ready now to face my fears and return to the city of angels that had been a real hell for me? I guess we would find out. The plane was leaving the next day, and I would be taking off to spend an adventurous one week in LA, two years later.

WEDNESDAY.
DAY ONE.

I WOKE UP in my lovely, and quite large, Bronx one-bedroom apartment around 8 a.m. on this particular Wednesday morning. I was too excited to sleep any longer. I forcefully flung the 300-count black Egyptian cotton sheets from on top of me down to the hard wood floor below. Now I was the one with the expensive sheets that I had dreamed about 2 years before when I was lying on that twin-sized bed in the first homeless shelter. The dream that became the prologue to my first book. The fantastical fantasy where the rock star and I had somehow managed to work everything out and we were finally happy together.

I'm glad that dream didn't come true.

My life had become so much more than I ever expected. And I was happy.

Happy.

It had been a long time since I could utter that word and actually mean it. But now, I could. Because it was true. I woke up every day excited about the possibilities that could unfold in each moment. Now that I was sober. Now that I had a secure place to live. Now that I was doing the things I loved to do and was surrounded by people who pushed me forward instead of those who constantly pushed me down. I was finally happy with my life and now I was about to board a plane back to the place where I had been living the extreme opposite of happy. The place where I had been miserable. The place where I seriously contemplated suicide. Would my newfound happiness survive in such a personally desolate place? There was only one way to find out.

I headed to the door, my luggage and trusty messenger bag carry-on packed to the rims. In my black suitcase, with the word WISDOM emblazoned on it, I had carefully packed new socks, new underwear, a new fancy grey button up shirt I would wear at my book signing, the suit that I had worn on the TV show "The Goodwife" when I had my breakout moment, my dress shoes and a couple of very "New York" style t-shirts, so that everyone would know where I was coming from.

I was proud to be a New Yorker now. The city had been tough on me that first year and a half, but when I had pulled myself together and changed my life, the city became my best friend and one of my biggest supporters. I had made it in New York. And you know what the song says, "If I can make it there, I'll make it anywhere..."

I requested an Uber at around 8 a.m., and the black Town Car arrived within 5 minutes. The nerves started to rise, and the memories of one of my last Uber rides flowed through my mind. But this time I wasn't going to be driven around on an all-day bender after hearing about the death of my grandmother. This time, the Uber ride was one to really celebrate. I had made such strides in my life since that fateful day two years prior. My grandma would be proud at how far I had come. I felt her energy, and my mother's, with me as the car traveled down the road towards the airport.

When we pulled up to terminal 3 at JFK International Airport, I took in the grandness of the buildings. The big automatic door in front of me seemed to call out my name, whispering of my big adventure to come. The driver came around to help me get my bag from the trunk and wished me well on my trip; just the beginning of the surprising VIP treatments I would receive throughout the day.

Next, I walked up to the Virgin America counter and was greeted by a cute, young, African-American girl.

"Hello! Where are you traveling today?" she asked with a smile.

"Los Angeles," I said bravely, trying to hide the fact that I was still kind of nervous about the whole trip.

"Fantastic! Going on vacation?" she inquired politely.

"Workcation, actually. A book signing." I said proudly, rummaging my bag to show her a copy of my memoir.

"Wow! You wrote a book? That's so awesome! So many people say they want to write a book, but never do. That's a big accomplishment! What's it about?" she asked.

"My life. The last three years. Hollywood, love, heartbreak, drugs, booze, rock stars, New York, homeless shelters, ego, sobriety, change and dreams finally fulfilled. In a nut shell." I responded quickly, not trying to hold up the line.

She held her breath for a second, held her hand over her heart, and then exhaled as she said, "Amazing. Sounds like you've been through a lot. I definitely want to read it! Can I take a picture of it, so I'll remember?"

She snapped a picture with her pink covered iPhone and handed the book back to me across the counter. "I hope you are really proud of yourself. I don't even know you, and I am!" she said, as she started to push some buttons on her keyboard. "Here. I bumped you up to priority. My little gift to you. Shorter TSA line and early boarding. Enjoy your trip. I hope it's magical!"

Magical. There was that word again. I flashed a huge smile and thanked her for the upgrade. I looked out the large airport windows with New York in the background and suddenly felt extra confident about the next 8 days. Magic was promised in the cards. I was ready to experience whatever the Powers That Be had in store for me.

The Priority TSA line was very short as she had promised. I think there may have been only 3 people ahead of me. When I pulled my black cowboy boots off to put into the bin, I had another flashback. Two and a half years ago, I abruptly had decided to leave my life in LA behind and escape to find myself again. The TSA line back then was very long. The memories of the drama that ensued because of my lack of proper ID, the fact that I looked hung over (which resulted in a pat down, search and questioning) raced through my brain now, as I set the bin on the conveyor belt.

This time, equipped with multiple forms of up-to-date IDs, with the correct spelling of my name, I had no issues walking directly through to the boarding area entrance. It was almost a shame I didn't get a massage-like pat down this time around. The TSA guy was pretty cute.

As I slipped my boots back on and put my iPhone back into my pocket, I let out a sigh of relief. I had made it in with no problem, and now, there was no turning back.

I stopped into the first coffee shop I saw and ordered a vanilla latte with a vanilla cupcake. I knew I would be tasting the familiar flavors at Hollywood Cakes very soon, so I guess it was like a breakfast homage paid in advance. The cupcake wasn't as good as the ones I used to make, though, and that got me even more excited about seeing my West Hollywood cake shop, Tim, and all the employees again. Some of the new employees I had yet to meet, but I had been talking with them over the phone for the last 2 years. So, I felt like I knew them.

I finished up at the breakfast spot and headed to the boarding area for my flight. I had arrived pretty early, so there was ample time to sit and think. I pondered all the possibilities and opportunities that awaited me when I finally landed safely, and soberly, back in LA.

Before I knew it, boarding had begun. My heart raced as I stepped into the ticket check line with the other priority passengers. Still tickled at how sweet the young booking agent was, I handed over my ticket to be scanned and strolled semi-confidently onto the plane.

When I found my aisle seat, 11 C, I situated myself in my chair and was surprised at the leg room available under the seat in front of me. I stretched out and closed my eyes for a brief second only to experience a flashback of the first time I tried to get on a plane two years prior when the Air Marshall and the cranky female flight attendant told me that I would not be able to fly with them because of intoxication fears, before quickly escorting me off the plane.

I came back to reality when a warm hand gently patted me on the shoulder. The male flight attendant, maybe in his 40s, had a welcoming smile on his attractive face as he politely asked me to make sure my seat back was up for takeoff. This was already 1000 times better than the last flight I had been on.

I buckled my seat belt when the announcement came on, but I don't think I was really prepared for the ride I was about to go on. As the plane took off, I thought about all the possible outcomes for every possible situation I might experience on the trip. Another side effect of sobriety: thinking.

Now that my mind was clear every minute, every hour, of every day, I was always thinking. I mean, I had always been one of those people with a big imagination and a stream of thought that was always flowing. I'm sure I came up with some "brilliant" ideas when I was drunk and high, too. But I never remembered those, and I don't know if any of them were actually legitimately good ideas, anyway. But now, all I could do was think. And feel.

There was no more hiding my emotions with drugs and alcohol. I had to face each one of them, in their truest forms. That's why, I think, even the littlest disappointments now felt so painful. And the slightest bit of good news seemed so joyous. Or maybe, I was always this emotional and just never realized it because my mind was always clouded. Either way, now I had to find some new ways to distract my brain from overthinking the possible results to all of my life's equations, so I could actually enjoy my life. Writing helped. A lot.

Miles in the air, somewhere over New York, I paid the fee for internet access, and received my first message from LA. It was Cheri, confirming the airport pick-up time. She was so excited to see me, and I was so ready to see her again. I missed her. I missed her a lot.

The further away from New York the plane got, I found it hard to believe that it had really been two and a half years since I had seen her and everyone else in Hollywood. It's funny how time seems to move by so fast at some moments, and then sometimes, it feels like time just can't move fast enough. Like when you are sitting on a plane. I wanted to be there already! To experience whatever magical adventure was waiting for me. I hoped the messages in the tarot cards were right.

A little over 5 hours later, the plane started descending into LAX International Airport. I thanked the crew for a lovely flight as I exited the 747 and headed towards the baggage claim. I messaged Cheri the second I stepped to the edge of the big silver luggage conveyor.

The text read: *"I've landed! Where are you, hubby? Did you bring a nice dress for the Beverly Hills jewelry store opening tonight?"*

I always called her my husband and she called me her wife. Probably the most stable relationship either one of us had back then, in the throes of our partying lifestyles. We always had each other's back. Except for that time I was homeless and decided I had to leave LA. She wasn't in a home of her own at the time, so she couldn't offer me a place to stay.

But she, like many other people, felt guilty now. Thinking they probably should have done more to help me back then. I didn't blame her. I didn't blame anyone, really. I was a pretty big mess, and

I wasn't ready to help myself at that point, anyway.

"Everything happens for a reason." Another quote from the proverbial THEY.

I never knew how true that statement was until I lived the craziest years of my life. At the time "everything" usually happens, you often ask yourself, "Why is this happening to me?" Because "everything" is usually hard to deal with, and you can't find any possible "reason" for the situation to be occurring.

It's not until time passes, and you find yourself at a better place in your life, that the difficulties of the "everything" make sense. And you realize it all had to happen exactly the way it did, so you could be exactly who you are today.

So, I'm not mad at my friends in LA for not trying harder to help me. Because they weren't supposed to. That wasn't part of the Creator's plan for me. Everything did happen for a reason, and I couldn't be happier with the end result.

The phone rang as I came out of deep thought. It was Cheri letting me know she had arrived. I gathered my suitcase and carry-on bag and hustled to the door as fast as I could. I could no longer over-analyze what could have been. It was time to finally face everything I had left behind.

Cheri jumped out of her silver Prius and ran over and gave me the biggest hug we had ever shared. When she let go, she gave me a look up and down and in her lovely English accent said, "Wow! You look so good! Healthy. Happy."

"It's so good to see you!!" I yelled back at her, not able to contain my excitement. "I can't believe it has been two and a half years!!"

The second I got in the car and we started to drive out of LAX, I looked over to see my beautiful, dark-haired friend, whom I had missed so much, and instantly, it felt like we had never been apart. Funny how time works like that.

Within minutes we were laughing and joking around like the good old days. I was so happy to be back in LA with her by my side. I already knew that things would be different this time. Because we were different. We had both grown up during our time away from each other.

Cheri was going back to school to become a hypnotherapist, performing Reiki healing and working her day job as an accountant. She said she had not been going out much, and when she did, she rarely had more than a drink or two. I was impressed. And I was happy. I'm glad some of my friends were able to move forward in their life in positive ways after I left.

I was starving at this point and I asked her to take us to Tender Greens, a salad restaurant in West Hollywood, for a light snack before I checked into my Airbnb. As we turned left onto Santa Monica Boulevard, the flashbacks started to roll in.

"There is the convenience store that Jackie and I used to buy our glass pipes in before heading to my apartment and smoking crystal meth all night. There's the hotel I spent many nights in at various parties and hosted a few of my own. There's the grocery store I bought my $2 bottles of wine at before getting drunk while teaching my cupcake classes. And speaking of... there is Hollywood Cakes." I remembered out loud to Cheri. Time shifted again. It felt like it had been decades since I had been there.

We drove past the cake shop and parked around the corner at the garage next to Tender Greens. We entered the clean, open-spaced restaurant and headed to the counter to order. I knew what I wanted! The same thing I had always ordered when I lived there before. Baby Spinach, Extra Goat Cheese and Extra Dressing, a side of mashed potatoes and a mint iced tea. Perfect!

Cheri and I sat down across from each other in the wooden seated booth, and I let out a huge sigh of relief. I had made it back. And nothing terrible had happened yet. The night was still young, though.

I called Tim on his cell phone and told him to come meet us at the restaurant for a quick hello. I didn't have time to actually go into the cake shop and have those moments yet. I still had to check into my Airbnb, get dressed up in my suit, and go to this Beverly Hills jewelry store opening that one of my New York actor friend's mother was hosting.

When I saw Tim walking across the street through the floor-to-ceiling windows of the restaurant, I felt like I was home. Seeing his familiar grey hair, the frosting covered t-shirt, and the warmth in his eyes made me happy. It had only been a little over a month since he had come to see me in New York City for my book release at Stonewall, but it was still very good to see him again. He was like my father, and this was like the prodigal son returning home. It was a big deal for all of us.

When he walked in, we shared a loving hug, and he sat down with us for a few minutes.

"How does it feel to be back?" he asked, looking me once over. "You look even better than the last time I saw you!"

"Aww, thanks, Tim. I feel really good. I think I'm actually happy for the first time in a very long time. I can't believe I'm saying that, but it's true. I'm happy with my life, I'm happy to be here, and I'm really happy to see both of you!" I said, stretching my hands out to rest on their hands.

"We really missed you around here," said Cheri, taking a sip of her iced tea and looking over to see Tim nodding in agreement.

Time had sped up a little and was now ticking back to its normal beat. We talked for a few minutes longer, and Tim excused himself to head back to the busy cake shop. I told him I would come in the following morning to meet everyone and see the old creative workplace.

Cheri and I finished our meals, and I opened the front-facing camera app on my phone to make sure I had no spinach in my teeth. I had spent a lot of money to get them back into good shape after the drama of the drug dealer attack over a year ago in the Bronx. I had grown comfortable in my skin once again and, even though I had a big scar on my chin, I continued to pursue my dreams daily.

I had a new outlook on life. Thanks to sobriety and everything that had happened in New York. I was ready to show Los Angeles the new me, but first I had to check into the place that would be my living quarters for the next eight days. Funny enough, it was just around the corner on Palm Avenue, steps away from the last apartment building I lived in before escaping to New York.

Cheri pulled up in front of the mod style building and helped me pull my suitcase out of the trunk. She parked on the opposite side of the street and walked with me up to the gated front door. In a silver lock box, I found the keys to the apartment. We entered the building and took the elevator to the third floor. I was expecting to meet the Airbnb host right then, but there was no one in the apartment when we walked in.

The apartment was quite large and decorated nicely. Big screen TV took up one wall and in front of it was a semi-circle white leather couch that looked very comfortable. The sliding glass door leading to the balcony let in a lot of light and I could see a bench out there, perfect for my morning smoke and writing my daily blog.

Yes, I was still smoking at the time. I hadn't been ready to quit that habit just yet. I mean, I gave up booze and drugs over a year ago, but I felt like I had to keep one vice or I would cease to be me. An absolutely ridiculous way of thinking. Something about smoking seemed a little harder to give up. I would give it up eventually, but for now it seemed to be only solace when the unavoidable stresses would arise. The lesser of three evils but still bad for me.

I didn't have time to even think about smoking at that moment, though, because it was time to get changed into my suit for the Beverly Hills event. I had packed my first evening in LA full of exciting adventures, sure to remind me of the good I had left behind. And maybe, to show me what my life could have been like in Hollywood had I been able to get sober back then.

So, I got dressed up into my silver suit in the large, very neat, suite. Fixed my hair in the mirror as Cheri sat on the king-sized bed and played with the large plasma TV hanging on the wall. This was definitely hotel quality living! Back in the bathroom mirror, standing in front of me, looking back with his clear blue eyes and clear skin, was the boy who came to Hollywood all those years ago. Full of dreams once again and ready to take on the world. This time with a powerful and inspiring message.

We left the apartment and drove down Santa Monica Boulevard towards the fancy jewelry store opening event. When we passed the big Beverly Hills sign that sits in a grassy lawn across the way from the entrance, I felt a momentary bit of pride rush over me. From the New York City shelters to a swanky Beverly Hills party. It felt good to be back on top.

We stopped off at Wolfgang Puck's restaurant nearby to share an ice cream sundae and two cups of espresso. Boy, did we feel classy. That feeling of elitism lasted for about 5 minutes before I started putting whipped cream on the corner of my mouth and pretending it was something naughty. We burst out in laughter, not caring what anyone around us thought.

Husband and wife were back to their old, comical ways. Except this time, there was no need for alcohol or drugs. The joy and laughter provided us with all the high we needed. I was so happy to be back.

Before we left to head to the event, we both stopped off in the restrooms. When I entered the stall, I was slightly shocked when the toilet seat rose on its own. I giggled as I looked to my right and saw a silver control panel. The buttons read: *seat warmer, rear cleanse, front cleanse* and *air dry*. You know I had to try them out! Unfortunately, mine didn't work. But when I came out of the bathroom, Cheri informed me that hers had worked. And she enjoyed trying them all. We laughed pretty hard at that one before gathering our senses and returning to our fancy "adult" attitudes.

A few doors down, the grand opening party was underway. We stepped onto the pink carpet and took photos with the provided jewelry themed props. We were offered champagne, but we both turned it down. Seemed like Cheri had decided to join me on this sober adventure. I couldn't have been happier with her decision.

We said goodbye to the hosts and made our way back to the car. Cheri informed me she had been sober for three days prior to my arrival. That brought some extra joy to my night. Knowing she would be going out with me and not drinking made my life a little easier. One less temptation.

We drove down Sunset Boulevard towards Book Soup, where my book signing would be held that Friday. I asked her if we could stop, so I could see if they had put my poster up in the window. She parked, and we walked a block down to the brightly lit up bookstore. The "bookseller to the great and infamous," as the sign above the shop read.

There, in the large, street-facing display window, directly adjacent to the entry door, was my sign hanging proudly, with a copy of my book underneath. I stepped back, and then forward, then back again, barely able to believe my poster was hanging in that window. The window where the posters of so many famous authors had hung to promote their events. Spike Lee had been there two weeks prior. I was definitely in good company.

I decided to order us an Uber to take us to our next destination because parking around the crab place was always a nightmare. But before I did, we walked a few buildings down to The State Room, the hub of all my heartbreak, broken dreams and ultimate betrayal, but also the place I had some good times, and made some of the most important long-lasting friendships of my lifetime.

We stepped into the side door to the cigar bar, and it was like time had stood still in this place. Two and a half years later, and it still looked exactly the same. I think maybe they had put one new TV up over the door, but that was it. Same floor-to-ceiling wood paneling. Same old-school cigar lounge seating and heavy wooden tables. And same old bartender, who wasn't old in the age sense, who had worked there when it was another bar.

Lex was a Spanish guy who had always been really nice to me. Except for the times when I would get out-of-hand drunk, and he was forced to kick me out for a while. He was even working the last time I got kicked out of The State Room. (The time when I was harassed by some straight guys for being gay and "looking at them funny." When I jumped onto the wooden table and threw the contents of my drink out onto the aggressors as my buff friend Jake and Lex forcefully removed the two men, before they could actually hurt me.)

He didn't recognize me for a minute.

When he finally figured it out, he got visibly emotional. A huge smile stretched across his face as he ran around the bar to give me a strong hug. "Wow, wow, wow! Look at you! Amazing! Healthy. Handsome. Happy," he said, as he patted me on the back after finally releasing me from his bear hug.

I filled him in on the past few years kind of quickly, and he was so happy. And proud. "You really did it. I knew you always had it in you," he stated. It was really good to see him, too. He was always one of my favorites.

We said goodbye and ordered the Uber for our ride to Hot N' Juicy. I told him I would be back to take him up on the nonalcoholic beer he had offered before I left LA. I didn't really know what my schedule was going to lend time for at that moment, but I had a feeling I'd be back at The

State Room a few times before the trip was over.

The car arrived, and we were on our way. I had been craving those particular crab legs since the day I left LA. There was something about that place. The food was amazing, of course, but secretly I was hoping that Tad, the handsome manager, might still be working there. He would be a sight for sore eyes, for sure.

When we entered the crab place, I was relieved to see that it, too, was exactly the same as I had left it. Except for one thing. Tad no longer worked there. Darn it. I was kind of hoping I could give him a copy of my book so he could read about how I felt about him back then and how much I appreciated the VIP treatment he always gave us.

We were seated in the back booth, one we had sat in many times over the years. I didn't recognize any of the faces of any of the servers. We sat across from each other and briefly looked at the menu to jog our memories on our favorite orders. We remembered quite quickly and called for the waitress to come over.

A dark-haired girl came from the back and it was actually someone I remembered! It took her a second, but she realized it was me and was so happy to see me. The VIP treatment ensued. But instead of free glasses of wine, she comped our drinks and gave us free corn. Not a bad deal, for two sober friends who were hungry and on a budget!

We chatted as we put on our lobster-embroidered plastic bibs and gloves in preparation for the meal. I could already taste the warm crab meat in my mouth when I saw the buckets coming towards our table.

Flashbacks of conversations with multiple friends, on multiple occasions, sped through my mind. I picked a crab claw and held it across the table, like the one I had pointed at Cheri years ago when she had come clean about her past relationship with the rock star I was involved with at the time. Funny how some physical things can make you vividly remember a moment in time.

The memory faded as we ate and talked about the adventures that lay ahead in the week to come. We confirmed all the plans that we had together while we finished our meal. Upon receiving the bill, I decided I would leave a copy of my book for the owners and the staff. I had written about it, and it was one of those places that meant so much to me. They definitely deserved a copy.

I signed it and handed it to our server. She smiled and told me she would make sure the owners got it. I also was able to coax out of her, quite easily, Tad's last name and Facebook page. I wanted to let him know about my book signing. Maybe he could come, and I could give him a copy of my book then. It was a nice thought.

We left, stuffed like a crab, and happy. A new Uber driver picked us up outside of the restaurant and drove us back to my Airbnb. Cheri stayed in the car so that she could be dropped off at home. We shared a kiss on the cheek and a big hug before I exited.

I took the elevator to the third floor and quietly opened the front door to the apartment. I was hoping not to wake the host if she was sleeping. It was around midnight or 3 a.m. New York time. I was absolutely exhausted. But it was the best kind of tired ever. When I hit the comfy bed, all I could think was what an amazing first day back in Hollywood it had been. Magical, really. I had high hopes that it would only get better from then on out. I fell asleep quickly; I couldn't wait to see what would happen next.

THURSDAY.
DAY TWO.

I WOKE UP early on my first morning back in Los Angeles, 6 a.m. to be exact. I don't think I had ever seen the sun in LA from that side before. Usually, the last year I lived there specifically, I would have been just going to bed or wide awake in the middle of an all-night crystal meth smoking party. It felt really good to be on the other side now.

Speaking of the sun! It shone through the silky see-through golden curtains, illuminating my face just enough to politely wake me up. The warmth of the Hollywood sun seemed to feel different from the one in New York. But I quickly realized, it wasn't the sun that felt different, it was me.

I jumped out of bed and headed to the spacious and very clean private bathroom. I splashed my face with the chilly water and then tried to start my daily shaving and beautifying routine. Remembering I had just been on a plane 12 hours prior, I realized I would have to go and get all the needed liquid products that I couldn't pack: shaving cream, facial lotion, deep cleansing wash and some various other beauty products.

I dusted a little bronzer on my face as to not scare the locals with my blinding New York whiteness. I was hoping I would find a few hours in one of the days I would be in LA to escape to the pool and get a little bit of color. I can't even remember the last time I had lain out by the pool or swam. Stuff like that hadn't made it into my NYC lifestyle.

Bronzer on, I quietly exited the apartment, feeling a little more like a West Hollywood resident once again. The sun looked and felt even better once I got out into the world. The air seemed much cleaner than I remembered, and the palm trees all around were a sight for sore eyes.

At the end of Palm Avenue all the familiar images were now physical, not just a fading memory I held onto for the two and a half years I was in New York. Not much had changed. The yogurt shop where I had set up a business partnership between the cake shop and the two lovely female owners was still the same. The car wash that was always busy and the small walk-up window hamburger joint that sat next to it. To my right, was the path towards the strip of gay bars where I had experienced many good times, (but probably more bad). And to my left, the path that led to the cake shop and another mix of emotional baggage.

I headed to my left. The CVS drug store at the end of the street was that way. So, I began to walk and memories floated through my head as I strolled. How many times I had walked this path in the years that I lived in LA? At least a million? How many people had I met on those streets? In this neighborhood? I was sure to see someone I knew on this morning walk. The person I would run into would prove to be totally unexpected, though!

I approached a familiar sign. Coffee Bean! Oh, how I missed it. In between Palm and the cake shop sat the coffee shop I had also visited probably a million times. Maybe not a million but definitely in the upper thousands! I entered with anticipation. "Large White Chocolate Dream Ice Blended," I said, before the gentleman at the counter even had time to say hello. He smiled and pressed the buttons on his screen. I tried to put my card into the chip reader but he waved and pointed to the slider side. Damn, these credit card machines are so confusing now. I thought technology was supposed to make our lives easier?

When I finally got my receipt, I headed over to the waiting area and began to scan the room for possible familiar faces. The man sitting on the maroon lounge chair sipping his latte from a mug looked sort of familiar, but not someone I had ever talked to. The blonde girl on her phone was definitely new in town, or new to me, anyway. But when my eyes reached the condiments bar, I saw her. Velma.

Velma was a heavyset African-American woman who rode around in a motorized wheelchair. She had a sweet face but the mouth of a sailor and a voice that reminded me of Miss Meyers in the first homeless shelter I lived in. High pitched and hard to understand. But I understood her. Most of the time. Even back when I lived in LA, I always took the time to say hello, listen to her, and help her when I could.

I don't remember exactly how I met Velma all those years ago, but it must have been on one of the nights after drinking at one of the gay bars on Santa Monica. That's where she usually hung out. I remember sitting down and talking to her, joking with her and thinking to myself how hard it must be to be homeless. I don't think I ever looked down on her, but I wasn't as empathetic as I was seeing her now. I had lived that life for a year and a half. In New York fucking City. I got it now. I got her even more now.

I walked over to her, and her face lit up when she recognized me. She got up as much as she could to give me a big, sloppy hug. It was good to see her again, too. We went out onto the patio and talked for a little bit. I showed her a copy of my book, and she said she was very happy for me. "You were always one of the good ones," she said with her twisted, but sweet, smile.

She told me she wanted to write a book, as well. She told me she was saving up money to get a new place. The same sort of things she said for years when I lived here before. But this time instead of just smiling and nodding I said, "if you really want something, go for it! I pulled myself out of a pretty deep hole. It is possible. It's never too late to take a chance on yourself and try."

She gave me half a smile and then asked me if I could help her out with some money. I gave her a big hug, some cash from my pocket, and told her it was good to see her again. Then she wheeled off to the right. Down the path to the gay bars. Or maybe she was going to the big grocery store down there. Either way, she was gone, and I definitely felt like I was home at that moment.

I continued my walk down to CVS to gather all the necessary face products. I passed by the cake shop and saw that no one was there yet because it was still a little too early in the day. I would go by there later, once I had my face shaved and was put together properly. I wanted to make a good impression on the new staff and maybe flirt with the guy who took my job. It was like the prodigal son returning home, so I wanted to drum up the suspense. I've always been a fan of the drama.

The walk was great. Even though I usually walked about 6 miles a day in New York, this walk seemed very long. But I got there, got the supplies and headed back towards the apartment. I stopped off for a quick breakfast at the kitschy 24-hour diner-style restaurant that was next to the bank. Boy, did I have some memories here. Kicked out a few times, too. They served the best pink creamy cocktails, and I had my share back then. They played good music, too. So, you can't really blame me for intoxicatingly dancing inappropriately in front of diners, can you?

Breakfast was tasty and drama-free. I got back to the Airbnb apartment in a few minutes and sneaked into my room to get ready. Wash, rinse, shave, powder, bronzer, done. I packed my messenger bag with a copy of my book and headed to the front door. When I turned the handle, I heard a "hello!" coming from behind me. I turned around to see a cute, young Asian girl in exercise clothes waving at me.

"Oh, hi! Are you the host here? Mimi?" I asked, putting my bag on the table.

"No, I'm Diana. I live in the loft upstairs. Mimi is out at the moment, walking the dog," she replied, opening a DVD case that was in her hand.

I introduced myself and told her a little bit about my life. She did the same. Turns out she was a student at UCLA, one of the schools I would have tried to go to, if my mother hadn't died my senior year of high school. I told her how cool it was and wished her good luck on the new school year. I told her I would leave a copy of my book in the apartment if she wanted to read it on her breaks. She agreed happily. I took the copy out of my bag and handed it to her before I headed out the door. What a nice girl!

Next up was the cake shop. I had mentally prepared for this moment the whole morning and really, the past two and a half years. I couldn't believe it had been so long since I had stepped foot into the bakery where I had spent almost every day for 9 years. When I walked in, it, too, was pretty much the same but with a few upgrades. Two of the new girls, Angie and Rebecca, greeted me with an excited hello and big hugs! They knew who I was immediately. They had been seeing my face daily on books and posters that Tim had displayed in the store. And they recognized my voice from all the calls over the last few years. They were delightful.

The ladies went back to their individual cakes as I took my old seat at the front desk to wait for Tim to arrive. Like clockwork, he entered the narrow doorframe at 9 a.m. on the dot, carrying a big bag of powdered sugar. It was good to see that some things never change.

Not too far behind him was the familiar face of Marc, one of the designers I had worked with for years. He was a sweet guy, most of the time. In the past, we would go out to the gay bars occasionally and try and get into trouble. He knew a thing or two about fleeting fame, like me. He had been the star of a reality wedding cake show years ago, before working at Hollywood Cakes. It was so nice to see him again. "Hey, Bitch!" I said to him as I gave him a big hug. "Hey, Slut!" he responded, as he had done every day for the span of the time we worked together. It was good to be "home."

I answered a few phone calls, made some chocolate-frosted cupcakes for the bakery case, and took a cake order for someone purchasing a cake to be served at a book signing on Sunday. I thought it was pretty crazy that the one order I happened to take was for someone who was also doing a book event. Odd. Magical?

As much fun as I had, I knew I had many more things to take care of before my own big book event the following day. I was saying goodbye to everyone when the guy who replaced me at the shop walked in. Tall, good looking, long dirty blonde hair, nice body... totally my type. Uh oh.

I had talked to him many times over the phone during the years I was away. We always had flirty conversations when I called the shop and sometimes exchanged suggestive text messages. When Max walked in, he came up and wrapped me in his muscular arms for a big hug. It felt like I knew him. It was comfortable. Nice.

We flirted for a little bit as we walked down to the coffee shop to get his daily caffeine fix. I playfully held his hand as we strolled. It was very sweet, but I didn't make too much of it. I was only going to be there a week; no sense in trying to make something happen. Plus, I had another dirty-blonde haired man to worry about seeing: Liam.

We headed back to the shop, and I gathered my stuff, said my goodbyes, and headed out the door planning to head to the West Hollywood Chamber of Commerce to say hello to the President. I got about half a block away when I realized I didn't have an extra copy of my book in my bag. I ran back into the cake shop, grabbed a book and held it up as I jokingly said to the staff, "You never know, I might run into a big celebrity today and have to give them a copy!" Everyone laughed, and I walked out, excited to start my first full day back in the city.

I took a walk up to Sunset Boulevard and headed in the direction of the Chamber. An alternate route, so I could see some old stomping grounds along the way. The first place I went to was Saddle Ranch, a country-themed bar and restaurant complete with a mechanical bull in the middle. I had been kicked out of that place many times in the past, too. "Dancing obnoxiously" and "bothering people" in my drunken stupor were usually the reasons.

I settled up to the bar and was pleasantly surprised to see a bartender that I knew. Tall, short blonde-haired, British gal who had been there for years. When she recognized who I was she seemed to get a little nervous at first. Maybe I had been a mess the last time I was there, but I didn't remember. She said, "Hello, there! Long time no see. How have you been? What have you been doing?"

"Sober. I've been sober for a year and two months," I said, chuckling a little, flashing a smile, and holding up my book. "And I've been doing some pretty amazing things!"

Her demeanor changed immediately and with a light in her eyes now shining, she said, "Wow! You definitely look healthy, happy and handsome. Sobriety is working out for you." I ordered a nonalcoholic beer, and we talked for a good thirty minutes. I told her a quick summary of what my last two and a half years had been like. She, like everyone else, could barely believe it. "I'm happy you made it through all that. Welcome back."

I finished my faux drink, thanked her, and headed back out of the completely wooden complex onto Sunset Boulevard. I decided to order an Uber to take me to the Chamber of Commerce because it had started to get a little hot outside. Cali weather was nice though, compared to the constantly fluctuating patterns we had in New York.

It wasn't but a five-minute ride down to the Chamber office on Santa Monica Boulevard, and I got there excited to see my old friend. She wasn't there. But I did find out there would be a Chamber mixer event the following Wednesday. My last night in town. It would be nice to go and surprise everyone with the new sober, author, actor, successful version of myself. I told Cheri via text that we had to go make an appearance. She agreed.

I really hadn't planned anything else for the day, so I decided to go to The Abbey for a light snack and a virgin drink. I also wanted to check out some men and see if any of my old drinking buddies, or bartender friends, were there. I arrived pretty quickly via another $5 Uber ride and entered with confidence. Again, I didn't remember the last time I was there and wondered if I had gotten in trouble. Either way it shouldn't matter. I was a changed person. I was sober, and I was spreading a good message. They couldn't possibly hold anything against me now, right?

When I sat down in what used to be my normal spot at the bar, I was happy to see a very sexy bartender friend of mine. Shirtless per usual. I think it's in their contract to work shirtless, and I didn't mind. It took him a few minutes to come over to my side of the bar, and even after he saw me it took him a little bit to recognize me.

His eyes lit up, too. This was becoming a common occurrence. One I really started to like.

Nate came up, grabbed my hand, shook it and kind of hung on to it for a second as he looked me up and down. "Damn, man. It is so good to see you. You look great! Super healthy and happy. It's so strange, just last week I was thinking about you. I was looking at my favorite picture of me, that you took... and I thought, I hope he's not dead." He said, looking at me with a clear sign of relief on his face. He let go of my hand, smiled and continued, "I'm so glad you are not. Where the hell have you been? And... what can I get you?"

I ordered a virgin Mojito and retold the story of the last few years, showing him my book and a multitude of photos from Facebook. When he saw the pictures of my TV gigs, my off-Broadway show, and my comic book appearance, he beamed with pride. "I always knew you had something special in you. The booze was keeping you down, man. Congrats."

We chatted for a little bit longer. I also saw a regular customer and his little Chihuahua who I had many conversations and drinks with in the past. We talked for a bit and he, too, was surprised at my crazy adventures in New York. All in all, it was a wonderful return to the gay scene in West Hollywood, but I still had other places to visit.

I said goodbye and headed out through the church-like iron gates, sober. And happy. I'm not sure I had ever done that at The Abbey before. It was a good feeling. It felt even better that the dark voice of temptation had been very quiet so far this trip. I had come a long way up to this point. It didn't seem like anything could bring me down now.

I made my way back up to Sunset Boulevard and headed to the Twisted Rainbow, the rock 'n' roll Mecca where stars like Ozzy Osbourne and other rock legends frequented. The place where, on my last night in LA, I gave a heart-wrenching performance of the song "Creep" before getting my heart ripped out of my chest by the rock star later that night and eventually deciding it was better to fly to NYC than to kill myself. Yeah, the place held some memories. Some very dark ones, but some good ones, too.

It was on this walk that I got a text message from Jane, one of my dearest LA friends. Jane and I met through a mutual friend at a house party one evening back in the day. A night surrounded by music and booze, where the two of us sparked an instant connection. She texted me on this day to say welcome back and that she was so excited to see me again! I was beyond excited to see her, too. We kinda had a falling out that last year I was in LA, and she had some issues of her own. She told me she would be coming to my event the next day and going out with us after. I eagerly awaited this reunion.

I put my iPhone in my pocket as I reached the driveway to the iconic Twisted Rainbow. Rock posters, personal photos of rock stars and memorabilia hung on every wall of the patios and inside. The flashbacks started racing when I stepped foot inside, but I held them at bay for the time being, so I could live in the moment.

This was another one of those places that never seemed to change. Same bar stools, same bar tables, same ash trays and, thankfully, the same female bartender. Cynthia had worked there for a while, or at least since I had started going there a few years ago. She was a voluptuous Spanish gal with big bosoms and an even bigger personality. She currently had her dark black, shoulder-length hair streaked with some neon pink and green. Very rock 'n' roll. Very her.

It took her a few seconds to recognize me, the same way it had been happening all day. Did I really look THAT different? I guess I did. I had forgotten how much weight I had lost when I was using all those drugs and surviving on a boozy liquid diet.

"God! You look so happy, healthy and handsome! So glad to see you in person and not just in posts online. I was worried about you that first year..." she said, coming around the bar to give me a hug. I was worried about me, too, back then. Glad all of that is behind me now.

I had another faux beer, and we dished the latest gossip like the old days. I thought of asking her about Liam, but I decided not to. I had read online that he would be out of town performing in Texas until the 28th. So, I knew I didn't have to worry about any run-ins until then. That took some pressure off of my upcoming event. And really, it took pressure off the whole trip up to that point. But if the tarot cards were correct, I would definitely see him before I left LA.

I said farewell to my friend and told her I would be back before I left town. She smiled and waved as I exited the famous rock 'n' roll bar. Once back on Sunset Boulevard, I decided to head in the direction of The State Room. Maybe see if I could run into more of the people I had not seen in two and a half years. This trip was all about facing fears, and making amends. I had to put myself in those possibly scary situations in order to test my new-found character, and in some cases, get some long-awaited closure.

Walking down the Sunset Strip, past the empty building where the "almost" yoga studio and charcuterie restaurant used to be, the flashbacks of those last few weeks in LA, before I left for New York, came rushing back through my mind. Visions of the yogi who had allowed me to move my furniture into his yet to open yoga studio, when I found myself evicted from my beautiful West Hollywood apartment. And when he found me dressed as Sarah Summers, three days later, playing video games with friends and kicked me out in a freaked-out fit.

The building next to it was where I had met Wendy and Leah, the two beautiful restaurant owners who had saved me from living on the street by allowing me to sleep on the floor of their office while helping them out in return. Wendy's last-minute rush to get my computer and a few beauty products to me at the Hilton LAX via messenger, before my plane took off, over two years ago.

Good memories. And bad memories. But now, just memories, as I slowly walked by these two, now closed, businesses. Just looking at them again, I felt bigger now for some reason. Or the buildings seemed smaller? I guess, it was because they didn't hold any power over me anymore. I was a better, much stronger, person now. But I was thankful for everything, and everyone, in my past. Because it all led me to this beautiful life I was leading now.

I continued to walk towards The State Room when a little commotion in front of me caught my eye. Four paparazzi were hovering around the front windows of the Subway sandwich shop. It tickled me a little to see them. I was definitely back in Hollywood.

As I came upon the scene, I suddenly got a craving for some chocolate chip cookies. And let's be serious...I wanted to see who was in there getting lunch!

I slid passed the paparazzi and entered the very narrow two-table restaurant. There was only one person besides me in line and it only took me a second to recognize him. Standing there in front of me ordering his food was one of the biggest celebrities in the world. Justin Bieber. Dressed in camo cargo shorts, a white t-shirt, with tattoos covering his nicely defined arms and a few on his neck, looking strikingly handsome with his newly buzzed haircut.

Instantly the 12-year-old girl inside of me got very excited! He was so cute in person! I wanted to squeal and jump all over him! But the adult person on the outside of me, who had worked with and been very close to many celebrities over the years, decided to handle the situation calmly and with respect. When he looked over at me, I nodded and greeted him with a, "'sup?" Haha. Trying to act cool.

He ordered his 12-inch sub meal, which included chips, cookies and four miniature bottles of milk. I watched him as he took his credit card from his pocket and put it into the card reader. I started to order my cookies when I noticed him taking his card out and putting it back into the machine. A frustrated look briefly washed over his face.

"I'm sorry, sir. Your card has been declined," the employee behind the counter said, looking kind of shocked. I thought it was a little strange, too, I mean didn't he make like sixty-five million dollars this year? Then I remembered how many times I had issues with my debit cards when traveling or when the bank thought something suspicious was going on and knew that he must be facing that issue.

"I'm gonna have to go to the car and get another card..." he said, as we both turned around to see a larger swarm of about 20 paparazzi now stationed outside the door waiting for him. In that instant, the voice of goodness inside of me spoke up and looking into his eyes I said, "Don't worry about it. I got it."

He tilted his head to the right and lifted an eyebrow. "Really? Are you sure?" he asked, like it was a big deal. First of all, it was a $16 meal. I would have done that for anyone in the same situation. And second, when I looked out and saw that the crowd of photogs had grown exponentially, I decided to save him from having to go back out there a second time to face them all without his food. I could already hear their loud, intrusive questions coming, "Where's your food? Did your card get declined? Are you broke?" Dumb stuff, but I knew how the celebrity game worked in LA.

I stepped up to put my card in the reader and he put his hand on my left shoulder, looked sincerely into my eyes and said, "Thank you so much. That's really cool of you." I smiled and at that moment something inside of me told me to invite him to my book signing event the following night.

"Hey Justin, I'm having a book signing and discussion across the street at 7 p.m. tomorrow night... if you are free," I said, pointing to the book store across the stretch of Sunset Boulevard.

"I'd love to, but I'm going out of town tonight," he replied, as he took the bag from the employee across the register.

Quickly, I grabbed the copy of my book from my bag and handed it to him. "How about something to read on the plane? I think you might like it. It's pretty inspiring."

"Yeah! Thanks. I'll definitely take a look at it. Good luck to you, man. And thanks again!" he said with a cute smirk, holding up my book and the plastic Subway sandwich bag as he walked out to face the horde of desperate paparazzi.

I watched as he made his way through the crowd of photographers, and I felt for him at that moment. He had just been so nice and so gracious. Not the rude, no-fan-photo-taking jerk the reports had been making him out to be lately. And then he had to walk out into all of that. The flashing lights and the screaming men asking inappropriate questions. Seemed like a lot to go through just to get lunch for his girlfriend and himself. It perplexed me how so much attention could be brought to some people. It seemed a little dangerous at times.

That was something I always thought I wanted. The fame, notoriety, paparazzi and all the glitz that followed. I had a little taste of it when I was doing the whole Britney Spears body double thing back in 2002, but it wasn't really the same. I wanted to earn it for something I did. And I wanted to be able to make a difference once I got the attention. Be an inspiration. I was happy to think that even in just the short few months my book had been out, it had already been helping people. And that's all I really wanted.

I finished paying for my cookies and walked out towards The State Room. Nobody stopped me or asked me any questions. I don't know if the paparazzi had seen me pay for his meal or not. And I was okay with that. I was happy with it being a random act of kindness between him and me. I decided right then and there that I wouldn't post the story on Facebook or anywhere. I would simply say that I met him if the photos of him with my book were to surface.

Walking down the street, I couldn't even believe what had just happened. I thought it would be okay to tell my closest friends, because I knew they could keep a secret. I called Tim immediately. He was flabbergasted. He said, "Wow, sounds like there is magic in the air! If those pictures come out, that would be amazing publicity."

Magic. There was that word again. So far the cards had been right. What else could possibly happen to top that?

I hurried into The State Room dining area where Ray, one of my favorite bartenders, was working. Recently back from a trip to some jungle location shooting scenes for his discovery TV show and back to work at the other job he loved so much. He, too, reacted in a similar fashion as everyone I had seen so far. A big hug across the bar and praise for how healthy and happy I looked. He still looked good, too. It was nice to see that he hadn't succumbed to the darkness that had been all around us back then. He was another face I missed a lot. I still kind of wished we had made that music video with Liam when we had the idea all those years ago.

He popped open a nonalcoholic beer for me, and we chatted about our lives. He had been keeping up with me via Facebook as had some of my favorite waitresses who had joined in on the reunion. They weren't expecting the Justin Bieber story, though. They were pretty amazed at what I had told them. They probably didn't believe it at first. But I wasn't one to lie about things. My life was an open book, and they knew that. I told them to be on the lookout for paparazzi pictures the next few days and to let me know if any showed up on any random websites.

As we chatted, my phone began to vibrate. It was Lacy, my pretend twin sister. She was super excited that I was back in town and invited me to a house party for one of her friends, a birthday party filled with free booze and the rock 'n' roll crowd types I used to associate with back at the Twisted Rainbow. This could be another test. Another temptation. But I knew I would pass with flying colors. Nothing was going to get me to drink again. I hoped.

Lacy came to pick me up a little before sunset, and it was another well-received reunion. So much love in the air. My fellow blue-eyed vixen smiled wide with her bright white teeth as she grasped me for a strong, minute-long hug. She was another one of those people who had known me forever. All the sides of me. She had seen me at my worst, but also at my best. When we were sitting in her car again, it felt like it had only been a day since we last saw each other. A clear sign of lifelong friends. I was glad to be back with her.

We went to her new apartment in Hollywood, and she gave me a mini tour of the place. It was very quaint and the perfect size for an actress making her way through the film world. I asked her if there was one available in her building, in case I wanted to move back. She said no, but that she would keep her eyes open for stuff nearby. I was thinking about it. Or if I had it my way, a bicoastal situation. Dream big, I always say!

We chatted for a minute and then her doorbell rang. It was our mutual friend Suzy, the beautiful, blonde, big-boobed, dancer who we had both known for a while! Years, actually. The last time we were all together was at another house party about ten years before. So funny how life works. Here we were again, going to a house party, but all of us in better places in our lives. No longer the struggling actors. We were adults. And it was great to reconnect.

The house party was a little lackluster for me, as I wasn't drinking, but I met a lot of really cool people. There was one moment, though, that I will remember forever. It just so happened that there were similar props at this party to the ones we had in that group picture from a decade ago. We couldn't resist the temptation to reenact the past and took an updated version on this night. Once we compared the two, it was crazy to see that all three of us looked younger, healthier and happier. It was beautiful. Suzy suggested that we start a tradition of remaking the picture every ten years. Lacy and I agreed.

I called an Uber about thirty minutes into the party to take me back to the Airbnb apartment. I was not only physically tired from the day's magical events, but I was mentally exhausted, too. I said goodbye to the girls, and Lacy said she would see me the next day at the book signing.

I made it back to the apartment and was a little surprised to see Diana and the host herself, sitting at the entry way table having a glass of wine. Before I could even set my bag down, the host introduced herself. "Hi, I'm Mimi! I think I know you! I think we know each other..."

The pretty Asian girl, with a sweet face and shoulder-length hair, did sort of look familiar. It was very possible that she did know me. That we had some sort of connection. I lived on that street for years and rarely left West Hollywood. I had a feeling when I booked the Airbnb that maybe I would know the person, but I didn't expect this story.

"Did you use to go to St. Felix bar? You'd come in and listen to your headphones and dance?" she asked, looking me up and down.

"Yea," I said, getting kind of nervous. My memories were vague about my nights on the town, but I did remember I had gotten banned from there. One of many places over the years. "It was definitely one of my favorite places for the short time I was allowed in there," I chuckled, trying to hide a tinge of embarrassment.

"I thought that was you!" she exclaimed. "Your name sounded a little familiar when you requested the room, but it wasn't until Diana showed me your book, and I read the back, that I knew it was you! You used to come in there all the time when I was working. We would talk sometimes. I never thought you got too out of hand, but you were definitely a character."

When she said that, I started to piece the past together. "Oh yeah! You were the host or the server or something... I really liked you!" I said. I hadn't really even thought about that place, but as we talked, it all came flashing back into my mind. I had really enjoyed going in when she was there, and it was so crazy that we ended up meeting again like this.

We talked for about an hour. She got pretty emotional as I told her my story. She almost couldn't believe it, and she shed a few tears as she said, "I am so proud of how far you've come. I always worried about you. I thought it was strange how you stopped coming around. But I'm so glad you are here now. It's amazing what you've been able to accomplish. I'm really inspired right now!"

I gave her a big hug and felt a little emotional myself. It's crazy to think that people only saw me as a drunk, hopeless, dancing mess for so long. I never saw myself as that person. But, when I look back, that was the facade that I put out there. That drunken mess hid most of my light for all those years. I was so happy to have this chance to show the world the new me. Or the real me. The person I was before the booze and the drugs creeped into my life. The person who had dreams and let nothing stop him from achieving them.

I gave the girls another hug and could barely get my boots off in my room before I fell asleep. The next day was my big book event. Was I prepared to face the crowd and speak my new truths to them? Would anyone besides my close friends even show up? I guess, all I could do was sleep and dream of what the next day would bring.

FRIDAY.
DAY THREE.
THE BIG DAY.

THE SUN woke me again on that Friday morning in West Hollywood. This time it was at a more reasonable hour, as I had gotten over the jet lag and time difference. I lazily rolled over and out of the bed. I wasn't trying to stress myself out before the event which was basically the culmination of all my hard work over the past year. Yes, it was a little nerve-racking, but it was a celebration of my personal triumphs, so I didn't let the nerves get to me.

I turned on my iPhone and opened up the Facebook app to make my daily morning post. I was fighting every itch inside of me to blast the story about what happened the previous day with Justin Bieber. I held out hope that some paparazzi pictures would leak before I said anything. I wasn't going to tell the whole story, so as not to embarrass him. But I was going to make note of his having my book if the photos came out. It made me think about how different my life would have been if social media had existed when Sarah Summers was at the height of fame impersonating Britney Spears.

I did have a website back then, though. When the Internet was just becoming a big deal. I taught myself how to manipulate HTML and had a pretty decent site where I would connect with fans who had seen me on Ricki Lake or read about me in the National Enquirer. Most of my fans were fellow female illusionists, drag queens, transsexuals and the men who liked them. I also had a fair share of gay followers, too. If social media had existed then, my life could have gone in a whole other direction.

But I'm glad things happened the way they did. I'm glad Britney Spears was part of my life back then and now. Always my spirit sister, she had a big day on this particular Friday as well. It was the release of her latest album. Coincidence? Or another strange cosmic happening, linking our lives together? The parallels continued. I didn't even think it was weird that the dates just happened to match up. It just kind of fit in perfectly with the way my life seemed to go. Magical.

Before I got ready for the day, I downloaded her new album, with the intent to find the perfect time to listen to it. After my event. My brain had to focus on what I would say that night.

I opened the door from my room to the living room, half expecting everyone would be asleep. But as I stepped out onto the patio, Diana and

Mimi said hello as they started their daily workout routine together. It was like having two really sweet roommates, whom I felt a real connection with. For my first Airbnb experience, it was A+!

I made my daily post sitting on the little wooden bench overlooking the clean West Hollywood street. A little note reminding everyone of my big book reading that night and teasing them with news of a big secret I was keeping; one that would be better revealed if pictures were to come out. The curious responses started coming in immediately.

I called Lacy and told her the whole story though. We had shared a lot of fun celebrity run-in experiences over the years, and I knew I could trust her with the secret. Told her to keep her eye out for pictures on the celebrity blogs that she loved so much. She told me how excited she was to come to my event and how amazing she thought the story about Justin was. Back in LA only two days, and I was already mingling with celebrities? It was good to be "home."

I spent some time at Hollywood Cakes in the afternoon and got to know the new staff a little better. It was crazy to see how much busier the bakery seemed to be since I had been gone. It pained me to think maybe some of my drunken actions in the past had cost the cake shop some business. I really loved that place like it was my own. Back then, everything I loved seemed to fall apart. I'm glad the cake shop was still standing and Tim was still in my life.

Time seemed to fly by that day. I left the shop a little before 5 p.m. to prepare for my event. Tim drove me, and about 30 copies of my book, up to Book Soup so I could help the staff there set up. The girls at the bookstore were very sweet and the room was put together in a matter of minutes. It wasn't a huge space, but I had high hopes I would have enough people in attendance to fill all the seats.

I told the ladies I would be back a few minutes before the event and headed down half a block to The State Room. I wanted to let them know I would be bringing people over after the event and to make sure I could RSVP my "special" table.

When I walked in, there were just a few people enjoying the early happy hour. It instantly reminded me of the old days, when it would just be me and Liam at the bar for hours at a time. Joking and singing. Before he hurt me. Before I found myself again.

I shook my head to loosen the thoughts and let them escape from my mind. I walked up to the bar and ordered my nonalcoholic beer, when I heard a woman's voice call out behind me.

"Kaleb? Is that you?!" said the smiling Spanish lady sitting at the bar-height wooden table behind me.

"Yes. Umm, hi?" I said hesitantly, trying to jog the memories of her face in my mind.

"It's me, Cathy!"

Oh yes. Cathy. Another one of my drinking acquaintances from Hollywood. We were never super close, but we always had fun together when we were both at the bar. She had been keeping in touch via Facebook quite often, and I felt like I got to know her more over the internet than I ever did in person. It was nice to see her face-to-face again.

Her husband sat down with us, and we had a lovely conversation about the past few years. They told me they were at the bar to have a drink or two before heading to my event.

At this time my text message alert started going off every other minute. Cheri, Lacy, Jane, and a ton of other friends, were letting me know of their arrival statuses. People were actually excited for this event, and that made me proud. It made me even more excited, too. And a little bit more nervous.

It was around 6 p.m. when I got a Facebook message from a friend in New York. The message read: "OMG! Look what he is holding!! You have to tell me the story!" I scrolled down a little to find a picture of Justin Bieber holding my book. Whoa! I froze for a moment and tried to let my brain catch up to the moment that was happening in front of me. The picture was proof that it wasn't just a dream.

I followed the link provided in the text message and found more pictures of the mega star holding my book. From many different angles. This was quite possibly the best free publicity one could ever ask for. Well, I guess, technically it cost me $16. But that was a magical number to me.

Justin Bieber had one of the biggest fan followings on the planet. If one percent were to take interest in my book, that would be amazing. I wrote my memoir to change people's lives. To help them overcome their hardest struggles. Looking at the multitude of paparazzi photos, I knew at that moment, my words would soon be reaching a lot more people. The people who needed those words the most. This was divine intervention if I had ever heard it! It was pure magic.

I opened up the Facebook app on my gold-encased iPhone and posted the photos with the simple caption: *"I'm just gonna leave this right here. (I'll tell you the story later) Justin Bieber is reading my book!"* Unfortunately, I had no time to write anything else. There was a huge book event down the street I had to attend. Mine.

I finished my faux beer and said goodbye to Cathy, her husband and the staff. I basically skipped down Sunset Boulevard back to the bookstore carrying a heavy bag of mixed emotions. Excited about the possible life-changing photos I had just seen, and nervous about the soul-bearing reading I was minutes away from performing.

When I walked back into Book Soup, Tim and Cheri had already arrived and were mid-sentence as I approached.

"Full house," said Tim, sarcastically, as he pointed around the room at the empty chairs.

It was only 5:30 p.m. at this point, but it did have me a little worried that the seats were still empty. Jackie texted me she couldn't get out of work.

Other friends, who had confirmed on Facebook weeks prior, sent messages that other things had come up. Would anybody actually show up for me? Or had I burned too many bridges in the past?

I paced around the room for a few minutes, twiddling my thumbs and playing with my hair, making sure it was as perfectly coiffed as could be. Finally, people started to trickle in. One by one, faces of my past came into sight. It had only been two and a half years since I had seen these people, but to me it felt like decades had passed. I experienced so much in those short years. Lived so many lives. And grew so much as a human being. But when I saw the faces of people from the different aspects of my life showing up, it was like no time had passed.

After the seats had been filled and others found their spots to stand, the time had come for me to speak and to introduce my old friends to the new me. The sweet Book Soup employee addressed the audience to get their attention as I waited off to the side. She then proceeded to ask everyone to silence their phones before introducing Tim. "Here is the owner of Hollywood Cakes, Tim."

Tim made his way through the narrow path between the rows of full seats. The audience, most who knew him, or had heard of him, applauded and smiled. He didn't seem as nervous as he did when he introduced me the first time at my New York City book launch event a month prior. He had his speech written down this time and felt more comfortable in a setting he knew well. West Hollywood.

He spoke of the tour of my New York life I had taken him on. He winced as he remembered aloud the neighborhood surrounding the shelters and how he didn't feel very safe. But then he beamed with pride as he spoke of the subway where I saved a man's life and the theater where I had my first off-Broadway show. He mentioned the questions he received by the audience in Manhattan. "They asked me, 'why did you stay by this guy?'" He ended the introduction by reading the eloquent foreword he wrote for the book. Part of it answered the question. "They say I'm just an enabler for his transgressions. But I've seen the latent potential just percolating below his addictive personality. I am the proud surrogate father to this prodigal son whose journey is still a work in progress. Ladies and gentlemen, Kaleb."

The audience erupted in loud applause, and I carefully stepped up to the podium. One that had been leaned upon by some legendary authors and celebrities before me. The slight tinge of nervousness I had been feeling disappeared when I moved the mic to a better position and looked out at the whole audience for the first time. The chairs were all full. And the space the bookstore had provided for the event was overflowing.

"Words have power."

My opening remarks.

"I don't think I realized how much power they had until I wrote them down."

I read the Readers' Favorite 5-star review and told the crowd how it made me tear up the first time I read it. After reading it, I talked about the reviewer. "This person, who has never met me, doesn't know my backstory and was touched in that way. It was then I knew my words had power. I'm so excited to continue on this journey."

I continued by talking about my daily Facebook blog and how proud I was that my posts were able to inspire people. How getting letters from people who I had gone to high school with, telling me how my journey motivated them to quit drinking or face their fears, made me joyful. I was beyond proud every time an old friend or acquaintance messaged me to let me know about their sober progress. I knew I was doing the right thing with my life in those moments.

I spoke of wanting to be an inspiration since I was a little child. How I always knew I wanted to be famous, but not for the money or the houses. But to touch people's lives and do a greater good in the world. I was so grateful that through my book, even with the few months it had been out, I was already able to effect change in the lives of others. It was a dream come true. A mission that I was so proud to be on.

"I told someone earlier that I've been listening to the most beautiful broken record I had ever heard. You look so healthy..."

I started to choke up at this moment. Because the next words out of my mouth brought tears to my eyes. I was speaking so openly and honestly. I let it all out.

"...so happy, and so handsome. I could listen to that song for the rest of my life."

The crowd smiled widely and chuckled with approval, as if they had felt every emotional nuance in those words. The energy in the room was so positive. I truly felt that I had come full circle since the events that led to all this had occurred. I WAS healthy and happy. More than I had been in over a decade. And it showed.

I told the crowd that just being sober wasn't the only reason for my youthful glow. Although it was a huge part of it. The glow partially came from finding my divine path. Knowing that I was doing what I was destined to do, gave me the strength and the courage to persevere.

I spoke of how I lost my ego in the shelters in New York City. The craziest, most difficult, year and a half of my life. I spoke of the friends I made in the most unthinkable of situations.

I read the chapter in which I quit drinking and using drugs for good, and the moments that led up to it. The uproar of applause after I read those words felt definitely earned. I had made a huge step in my life when I decided to give up drugs and alcohol. Things that I did every day. Dark things that controlled me and were embedded into my way of life. I gave them up. Cold turkey. It was a miracle, the things I was able to accomplish in a year. Or was it magic? Either way, I was grateful to be exactly where I was, and exactly WHO I was, at that very moment.

I finished the speech with a quote that was very dear to my heart. One that made more sense now, than when I first heard it 15 years ago. Words spoken by the one and only, Elle Woods.

I repeated her lines from the end of the first "Legally Blonde" movie, so eloquently spoken as she stood on the graduation stage at Harvard University, "It is with passion, courage of conviction, and strong sense of self that we take our next steps into the world, remembering that first impressions are not always correct. You must always have faith in people. And most importantly, you must always have faith in yourself."

The room filled with applause and my heart filled with pride. I had faced my fears head-on and emerged victorious. I stepped back from the podium, giving the slightest of bows, and then pointed in the direction of the back counter where I would be signing my book. I walked with my head held high, followed by the crowd of people.

These "people," my friends, former business acquaintances, my childhood pal from Texas, and my old bar buddies, formed a line that stretched around the room. It was so rewarding to see their smiling faces, patiently waiting for a signature, my book in hand.

My book.

It hit me right then and there, how real this whole thing was. I was a published author! With a real, physical book. A book that people actually wanted to read. One that some people had already read and had been touched by. Been changed, been inspired. And now, with the Justin Bieber photos out there, it was possible that many more people would find my words. Those words and their power. I'm so glad this wasn't a dream.

I took ample time to personalize each person's copy, and when Jane finally reached the front of the line, we both got a tad emotional. With tears in our eyes, we shared a two-minute long embrace. It had been far too long since I had seen her. Before Cheri, before Jackie, before Anna Lynn and Liam, there was Jane. She and I got into a lot of "trouble" over the years. But more on Miss Jane later.

When I finished autographing the last book, I told everyone of the after party at The State Room. Michelle, my cigar mentor, showed up towards the end of the event but told me she would be joining us at the bar. I was glad she came. I had actually seen her a few months prior when she stopped into a Brooklyn Cigar Lounge as part of her national cigar tour. But sharing a cigar, in the place where we first met, would be even more meaningful.

We packed up the few remaining books, but left five autographed copies for the store. I was hoping with the sales that evening, the book would make it to the top of the best sellers list. Having my book in the top ten of Los Angeles' most famous bookstore would be quite a feat.

I said goodbye and thanked the staff for the magical evening as we all walked out the door towards The State Room. The half-block path, one I had walked inebriated so many times, seemed like a victory parade. Because in many ways it was. It was crazy to think that two years before, just about any night of the week, I could be seen stumbling down this street. I was so happy that was in the past. The new me walked with pride now. No stumbles yet.

We gathered in the back of the lounge at the table where I had spent so many nights drinking and drugging with Liam and the gang. The flashbacks started pretty quickly, but I dismissed them just as fast. This time, one table would not be enough. I had a group of people who were happy to be seen with me and so proud of my accomplishments. It was something I had never felt at The State Room. Would have been nice to have this kind of enthusiasm when I had my cigar event there. Haha.

With three tables put together, we still didn't have enough room for all the people in our group. We pulled more chairs over and ordered appetizers and drinks. I had my nonalcoholic beer while everyone else had drinks. Cheri refrained from drinking that night, too. She was adamant on sticking to the sober life as well. And I couldn't have been prouder.

Michelle joined the table and sat next to me with a present. A robust cigar, like the ones we had smoked together in the past. It was nice to sit and talk with her in this familiar place, surrounded by people who cared about me so much. It was like no time had passed, when she properly cut the cigar for me and lit both of ours. Momentarily, I thought about how different my life would have been if I had not been such a mess when I lived in LA before. But then I realized, I wouldn't have met most of the people who were sitting with me at that moment. Everything happens for a reason. Looking around, I realized that even more.

Cheri got a text from an old friend saying that they were going to get some cocaine and wanted to know if we wanted any. The dark voice inside of me creeped in for a brief second. "Why not? You've been so good for so long... a little kitty won't hurt you."

I thought about it for a second, pretty seriously. But it wasn't too soon until the other voice spoke up, "Are you kidding me? You have worked way too hard to go backwards now. Especially here! At this place! Keep moving forward. I'm so proud of you." It was the undeniable voice of my mother. She was right. There was no turning back now.

I looked over at Cheri and just shook my head no. She laughed and said, "I can't even believe they would suggest that. Some people never change." She was right. SOME people never change, but some DO. And I was so proud to be one of those who did. I hoped to be a good example to some of the others sitting around me.

Tim talked with everyone and actually stayed until late into the evening. He and Lacy caught up. He spoke with my childhood friend and learned even more about my past. It was nice to see Tim outside of the cake shop and enjoying life. I was glad that the success of my book had helped him break out of his shell a little bit.

Sitting next to Jane and Cheri, looking across at Tim, Lacy and all my other dear friends, I felt a warmth of light and peace surrounding me. There was magic in the air. I couldn't have been happier. But there was one important person missing from the whole experience. Annette.

I had been wondering where she was, because she had told me a few weeks before that she would be coming. But with all the excitement and people, I had forgotten to text her earlier. When I finally remembered to reach out to her, it was too late in the evening. I decided to hold off until the next day.

The night ended with hugs all around. And I walked out of the bar happy...and sober. Any fears that I had were faced and obliterated. The new Kaleb was here to stay. There was only one person that could even remotely mess with my head, but he was not in town. This night was all about me. There were hardly any mentions of Liam at all. Thankfully.

I said goodbye to all my friends and made various plans with a few of them for the duration of my trip. When I entered the apartment a block down from the bar, I fell into bed, boots still on, and crashed. It was the best kind of exhausted a person could be. I don't remember all of my dreams that evening, but I vaguely recall envisioning Justin Bieber reading my book to his girlfriend on some private plane.

As I slept, I didn't know what the rest of the week might bring. But I had high hopes we had only seen the beginning of the magic. Turns out, I was right.

SATURDAY.
DAY FOUR.

I WOKE UP the morning after the big event with a huge smile on my face. The weight of the world felt lifted off of me in that moment, and I basked in the pure beauty of it. I had felt similar feelings a few times in the past, but this one was more powerful.

The mornings after my sold-out off-Broadway show and my official book release party at Stonewall were the closest in comparison. But this was different. This was a return to the place where so much darkness hard surrounded me, where I faced my fears, and now there was nothing but light.

I felt like I was flying, just lying there in bed. It was magical. The last few days had been nothing short of a fairytale and I was riding high on my white horse of triumph. The damsel in distress I had made myself out to be when I lived in LA was no more. I was my own personal hero, and it felt amazing.

All the people who showed up for me the night before were so wonderful. The conversations and the memories we shared. The pride that beamed off their faces in my direction was felt and appreciated. It was the perfect possible outcome to the equations I had been going through on the plane. But it wasn't one I expected. It was magic. I couldn't explain it any other way.

The Justin Bieber thing was, more than likely, divine intervention. But magical, nonetheless. I was reveling in gratitude to the Creator. My faith in The Great Unknown, and the faith in myself, had paid off big time. I wanted to stay in bed, wrapped in those feelings, but I knew I had to get up and continue to share the light with others. So, I did.

I pulled myself out of the comfortable king-sized bed as small rays of sunshine peeked through the curtain and made my way to the bathroom. It was nice to see the version of myself who looked back at me now. I could hardly remember the person I was before. But there were moments when I shaved my face or dusted on my bronzer, when I would have flashbacks.

Being so close to my old apartment didn't help those flashes from coming in that morning. I briefly saw the guy who smoked a glass pipe full of crystal meth and bathed himself in 'Fantasy' perfume, before heading to The State Room to fight Anna Lynn for the attention of the rock star he had fallen in love with.

When I heard Mimi's dog bark, I came back to reality. That imposter I had seen in the flashback was nowhere to be found. I took a deep breath, smiled at the new person in the mirror, and thanked God for my life the way it was now. I never wanted to go back to my old ways.

I stepped out into the living room and greeted the girls as they began their morning workout. I was definitely impressed, and inspired, by their daily commitment. Made me wish I could find some joy in working out. Maybe one day I would. Add that to the list of many things I wanted to do in the future. Right now, it was all about my book and my sobriety. My mental calendar was pretty full at the moment.

We said our hellos, and I headed out the door. It was another beautiful day in West Hollywood. The warmth of the sun enveloped me as I walked down the familiar palm tree-lined street. It felt like the birds sang for me as they joined me on a pink cloud of accomplishment. Nothing could bring me down. Or so I thought.

I decided to go to The Abbey for brunch. It was already full of people. I scanned the room for someone I knew, someone I wanted to show the new me to. I ran into one of the managers I had seen on the street the day before chatting with a few others who looked familiar. I went up to say hello and was taken aback by the conversation that proceeded.

One of the guys in the group asked, "How are you doing? Where have you been?"

"I'm great! I've been in New York City making a big change in my life. I'm over a year sober and here for a book signing. For the book I wrote," I said, showing them the book in my hand.

"That's all well and good, but, I remember having to deal with you all those nights. Kicking you out. You barfing in the plants, and once, on my damn shoes," the manager said, looking at me with a scowl. "I've seen this before. Somebody gets sober and writes a damn book. Then before you know it, they are back to their old ways. I don't know why we should have to deal with that."

BOOM! The train of compliments and good energy I had been riding on the past few days came to an abrupt halt with those few sentences. Who in the hell did he think he was, talking to me like that? Didn't he know what I had been through? What I survived to be standing in front of him at that moment?

No.

He didn't know any of it. And it took me a second to remember that. He hadn't read my book. He hadn't been seeing my daily Facebook posts. He hadn't seen me in over two years, and the last time he did, I was throwing up on his shoes, apparently. So, I couldn't really blame him for having that attitude.

"Well, obviously, you don't know me very well. I won't be falling off the wagon anytime soon," I said with complete confidence, as I smiled and walked away.

I started feeling a tad emotional when I walked out through those iron church-like gates this time. His words kind of stung. But they also made me think. I had been a complete mess. For a long time. There had been lots of people in my destructive path, and I hadn't taken into account how they might be struggling to accept the new me. Not just some manager at a bar I went to, but people even closer to me. People who had seen me try to get sober before. Were they still thinking it might all come crashing down around me again? That I wasn't strong enough to keep fighting this fight?

I hope not.

I'm pretty sure the people closest to me knew that when I put my mind to something, I made it happen. My mind was set on being a sober inspiration and leading a clean life. My real friends knew that. But I bet some of them had those thoughts after the first few months of my sobriety. "Is it gonna last this time?"

Walking down the streets of West Hollywood, having made no real plans for the day, I headed up to The State Room. There had been nothing but positivity thrown my way from that place since the day I got back. I thought maybe if I went there when it was relatively empty, I'd have some time to really think about the adventures from the days before. And who knows? Maybe my old friend Liam would show up and we could finally have that long-awaited conversation. One I had secretly been waiting to have since the day I left LA.

I walked in to the cigar lounge and headed to the far back wall by the windows where "my table" was situated. I hadn't seen a bartender, so I sat and waited patiently. I had been to that bar so many times, I really could have served myself. In the past, I wanted to be a part of the staff family so bad. I tried to help out as much as I could, even if some of the management didn't like it very much. I thought I really made some great connections with the employees over the years. I knew most of them cared about me, even if they had to kick me out a few times. A lot of times, actually.

When the bartender walked in, I was surprisingly happy to see him. This guy had been my arch bar rival when the football games were on. A tall, nice looking, Canadian guy who liked his Maple Leafs and loved the Seattle Seahawks. We hadn't always gotten along, but I did like him. He worked a lot and was always promoting the bar on his social media. I respected him for his appreciation of his job and his savvy self-promotion techniques. On this day, he was a sight for sore eyes.

"Jonah!" I blurted out when I saw his short, light brown hair come up from behind the bar.

"Kaleb? Hey! I heard you were in town. Wow, man, look at you. Looking good, buddy. Healthy, happy. What's up?" he said, coming around the bar.

"It's really good to see you," I said, giving him a light one-armed man hug. "I've been quite busy."

I told him stories of my life in New York and all the accomplishments I had achieved while sober. He popped open a nonalcoholic beer for me and listened as I told him my harrowing tale. Long gone were my top hats and Hello Kitty pocket mirrors filled with cocaine. It was nice to have a real conversation with my old friend and not worry about what might happen if I were to black out. Blackouts were something I didn't have to worry about anymore. A beautiful side effect of sobriety.

I went back to my table as Jonah continued to clean and prep the bar for the evening rush. I pulled out my NYU spiral notebook and began to write my thoughts. One of the things I wrote was a plan entitled "Things I Want To Do Next."

The list was comprised of seven things:

1. Book Signings in Texas and Boston. *(My hometown in Texas and at the Harvard Bookstore where my book was being printed and sold.)*

2. TV Interviews. *(I had done a public access show with my friend, Ginger, but I wanted to do a big news show, like the Today Show or Ellen, so I could reach more people to inspire and help.)*

3. Speaking Lines on a Big TV Show or Film. *(That was a goal I had on my list since I started taking my sobriety and my acting career seriously. I was hoping it would happen before the end of the year.)*

4. Trip to Another Country for a Book Signing. *(I was in talks with a printer/bookstore in Amsterdam about carrying my books. And, I had recently gotten my first US Passport, which had yet to be used.)*

5. Speak at a Sober Event. *(Inspiration is my purpose. I want to continue to share my story with people who are struggling to let everyone know what is possible through sobriety. Just need to find an event!)*

6. Set-Up Bicoastal Living Situation. *(A dream I had my whole life, but even more real now that I had seen how my life could be in Hollywood with sober eyes.)*

7. Movie Deal for Book. *(The biggest of all my new goals. My big dream. I had done so many things people thought I'd never do, maybe I could make this happen, too. Just had to meet the right people. Or win the lottery.)*

Seven goals. Seven new reasons to keep on my path. Some were bigger and harder to reach than others. But, if I stayed strong and continued to dream big, there's a good chance they would all be attainable. I just had to keep the faith in myself and The Great Unknown.

While I was writing, Lacy was sending me text messages. I put the pen down after listing my final goal and opened the messenger app. She was free for the evening and asked if I wanted to get together for dinner. I told her yes and to meet me on the Sunset Strip when she was ready. There were a couple more places I wanted to go that afternoon. Old stomping grounds I had to revisit on this trip of redemption.

Before I left The State Room, I had to use the facilities. Normally, going to the bathroom at a bar is no big deal. But this was no ordinary bar, and that was not just another bathroom. It was in that washroom that Liam and I had our first real emotional and almost sexual connection. I approached the big wooden door with slight hesitation. I knew that the second I stepped in there I would have some powerful flashbacks. And I was right.

The second my boot hit the slate grey colored tile, it was like I was two and a half years in the past. There he was. Tall, dirty blonde hair, glowing green eyes and his worn but handsome face, coyly smiling at me like he had been waiting there all day.

As I slowly approached the mirror, it was like I could feel him there, drawing me closer while holding a bag of cocaine in one hand and a key in the other. Standing body to body, package to package, the smell of "Fantasy" filled the room.

For a moment, I wanted it to be real. I wanted him to take me in his arms and tell me he had missed me. Tell me his life was not the same without me. Tell me that he needed me. Then I would finally give into him and fulfill those sexual advances he had made years before.

But it was nothing more than another flashback. I shook my head to wake myself from the vivid daydream and splashed some cold water on my face. I looked into the mirror and the sober reflection seemed to remind me that everything happened for a reason. I quickly remembered how hurt I had been but how that hurt ended up being the best thing that ever happened to me. Strange how the world works.

I exited the bathroom and paid for my tab. "Thanks again, Jonah! I'll be back."

The sun was making its way closer to the shore line, and it started to get dim on the Sunset Strip. But like clockwork, the lights of the rock 'n' roll bars seemed to turn on simultaneously. It was nice to be back. To be able to experience the famous street with a new clarity.

I texted Annette while I was walking but didn't receive an answer immediately. It was kind of odd not to hear from her for a few days, especially since I was in town for the first time in years. I got slightly worried but chalked it up to a probably busy schedule or something. I continued down Sunset Boulevard until I reached my next destination. Mel's Diner.

The famous 24-hour restaurant that had been featured in movies and TV shows over the years. A Hollywood staple as far as diners go. The place where rock legends would go to unwind after shows. And the place where I went for a coffee after I had my heart destroyed on a rather chilly evening in April a little over two years before.

I was kind of nervous when I walked in the front door. The last time I was here I was handcuffed and hauled off in a police car for snorting Splenda off a table. I didn't get arrested that night, but it was the last straw that became the catalyst for my move to New York City. I wondered if someone there might recognize me. Luckily, they didn't.

My mind was put to ease when the waitress, wearing a Tiffany blue diner dress, came over to take my order, and no cops were alerted.

"I'll have a coffee, please. I'm waiting for a friend," I said, politely smiling back at her.

I opened the yellow packet of imitation sweetener and poured it into the white diner mug that had landed in front of me almost instantly.

Their service was definitely good. I had missed this place.

I was enjoying the moment when I got the message that Lacy was close. I told her to pick me up at Mel's and then asked for my check. I walked to the cash register in the front and had a momentary flashback of the portly male cop guiding me out the door before handcuffing me in front of everyone on my last night in LA. Oh, how times had changed. I walked out this time, free as a bird, ready to continue my journey.

Lacy pulled up in her silver four-door sedan, and I hopped in, excited to have some alone time with my sister from another mister. This was the first time it was just us since the time she came to my apartment in the midst of my drugged-up days.

She had come over one evening, years ago, and I decided to get dressed up as Sarah, so we could take some pictures together. It was a fun evening, but I remember the look of disdain on her face when she saw me smoking the glass pipe full of crystal meth in front of her. I could tell it bothered her, so I continued to do it in the bathroom as the night went on. She was thinking about moving back to LA at that point, and I told her she could move in with me. But she declined.

I was a little hurt in the moment. Why didn't she want to move in with me? I wasn't any different than the person she knew before, was I? Of course I was. I was a complete mess. But I didn't realize it. I don't think any addict ever does.

Looking back, I completely understand why some people gave up on me. I wouldn't have been able to live with that version of me, no matter how good the intentions were. It made me happy that I was no longer that person. People actually wanted to be around me. They were offering me to stay with them now if I decided to move back to LA. It was worlds away from the situation I faced back then.

We had driven down the street just about a block when we decided on another restaurant-bar that I used to frequent in the past, once I was officially 86'd from The State Room. Church Key was the swankiest dim sum place I had ever seen. Lacy had never been there, so I decided to show her what it was all about.

We were seated in the middle of the spacious dining area, close to the free-standing fireplace that went floor to ceiling. Behind us, the long-rounded bar reminded me of the nights I had spent there. Drawing digital artwork on my tablet PC and escaping to the roof with new acquaintances to snort cocaine. Some of those memories weren't all that bad. I had some good times when I was there. It was usually when my mind went black that all the trouble happened.

After taking in the scenery, I sat across from Lacy and grabbed her by the hand. "It's so nice to be here with you. Like this. I'm sorry it took this long," I said, looking into her light blue eyes that were strikingly similar to mine.

"It's okay. All that matters is that you are here now. Sober. Happy and healthy," she replied, her eyes seeming to water a little. "Let's order!"

We ordered a charcuterie sampler and steamed pork buns. I also requested one of their fanciest nonalcoholic drinks, and Lacy agreed to having one as well. I told her she could have a drink if she wanted to because I wasn't one of those sensitive recovering alcoholics who couldn't be around liquor. I was a bartender on weekends in NYC, for goodness sake! But she decided not to drink during dinner and said she was proud of my strong sense of self-control.

A lot of people told me I have great self-control since I quit drinking. I do. But, it's because I know how much better my life is without alcohol and drugs. When I was in my drunken and drugged-up state, I don't think I could see that life ahead. I was under the control of the substances. Their dark voices kept telling me, "It doesn't get any better than this. Have another drink. Snort another line. You're a loser. You're alone. You'll never accomplish anything."

As soon as I shut those voices off, cut off their supply, my world started to change. The inner monologue was my own once again, and the good started to appear. For the longest time I used a hashtag in my daily posts "#thegoodiscoming." It was a way of trying to manifest it to be true. The day I moved into my first apartment after the homeless shelters and after the substance abuse ended, the hashtag read: "#thegoodishere." The good was all around me, and I only wished I had seen the light years before.

We chatted for a good hour or so. Lacy was dealing with issues of alcoholism involving someone she really cared about. It was nice to be there to support her with my hard-earned knowledge of sobriety. Selfishly, it was nice to hear that I was no longer the drunk that was causing her pain. But now, I felt for her in a different way. I could see the way the person was affecting her, and I hated the fact that I had similarly caused her, and so many others, that kind of mental anguish.

I lent my shoulder for her to metaphorically cry on that day, and I was proud to be this rock for her in her time of need. Our relationship had really blossomed since I quit drinking and using. I looked forward to making up for lost time while I was in town.

We finished our meals and thanked the staff as we decided on our next destination. Lacy told me that a friend of hers might want to meet us at the Twisted Rainbow and suggested we head there. I agreed. It had been years since I had been there at night, and I figured I might see some more people from my hard-partying days. People that I had missed dearly, and some I might even be able to inspire in my new form.

The moon was shining down on us as we walked the three blocks from the restaurant to the bar. It was like twin brother and sister back together again. Like the first time we went out when booze and drugs had not enveloped my life completely. Back then, we were two fresh-faced twenty-somethings with big dreams of making it in the city. Working at a fashion boutique on Melrose and craftily sneaking our way into the hottest Hollywood parties and clubs.

We even made friends with the paparazzi back then. They took our photos at night outside along with the real celebrities. We hosted some on-camera interviews for them, and at one point we both wrote for Celebrities.com. We had a spark inside us back then. On this night, sober and together, our light was back. We enjoyed the moment that had been long coming.

Walking up to the famous rock 'n' roll bar, cigarette smoke billowing from the patio, and the sound of electric guitars seemed to call our names. The nightlife was a tempting mistress. I thought how easy it might be to slip back into my old ways. But I was too strong for that. I didn't want to let anyone down. And most importantly I didn't want to let myself down.

At the entrance a big, butch, muscle-bound man stood with his back to us, chatting with someone behind the gate. I had a momentary vision of the many doormen I had encountered in my day. The many who would rough me up as they escorted me forcefully from random clubs. I smiled at Lacy and hoped this wasn't one of those guys I had pissed off in the past.

To my surprise, when the giant man turned around, it was someone I knew. Someone I had a history with. Jake! My old drinking buddy from The State Room. The one who had come to my defense when I was nearly gay bashed by two thugs on the night I was officially banned from my favorite bar. My hotheaded hero. It was good to see him, still looking as handsome as ever.

"Jake!" I yelled, grabbing Lacy's hand and pulling her to the front of the short line with me.

"Hey, buddy! Wow, look at you! Looking good. Healthy. Happy. Come here!" he said, stretching out his arms for a much-needed bear hug.

As we wrapped our arms around each other, I felt safe. He was a good man, and I was glad to see he was still around. We all spoke for a few minutes. Telling tales of the last few years and remembering some crazy nights from the past. He told me he had been keeping up with me on Facebook and was proud to see all the things I had been able to accomplish in a relatively short amount of time being sober. He let us in ahead of everyone else and told me, "if you need anything, I'm here. So good to see you. So proud of you."

We made our way to the upstairs bar where I was happy to find another familiar face mixing drinks. Kym was a lady I had met on one of my first evenings in the legendary rock 'n' roll bar. She was a spunky, black haired, thin, mature lady, who had a penchant for rocking the dark eyeshadow and lipstick. She always sort of reminded me of Elvira. She was known for her strong drinks and even stronger attitude. With me though, she was always kind. We connected in a very special way. Maybe she saw me like a son or saw the goodness that lay beneath my hard-partying ways. It was great to see her.

It took her a second to recognize me. I could see the thoughts going through her mind as she tried to piece together how she knew me. When she got it, it was like a small explosion occurred in her mouth. "Hey kid! Where the hell have you been? It's been a long time. What can I get you?"

I smiled when I said, "nonalcoholic beer, please." She looked at me kinda funny and then grabbed one from the fridge at the back of the bar. She popped the cap off and poured it into a chilled glass, handing it to me as Lacy and I sat down.

I told her my triumphant story and showed her a copy of my book. She took a step back as she held the novel and gave me a once over with her eyes. "I knew there was something different about you. You look really good. Really healthy. I'm so happy for you. You were always one of the good ones."

There were those words again: happy and healthy. This truly was like listening to a beautiful broken record, and this time it featured an electric guitar solo.

We chatted for almost an hour. At one point a song that Lacy and I loved came on, and we ejected ourselves from our bar stools into an all-out private dance party. It was still early in the evening, and the upstairs bar had no patrons besides us. That's how I liked it. It felt very VIP. And the dancing reminded me of the good old days with Lacy. When we first stepped off the plane many years before and our dreams were still fresh. Before the booze, the drugs and relationships tarnished our innocent spirits. We weren't thinking about any of that as we took turns videoing each other on our phones. It was pure, innocent and sober fun.

Lacy received a text from one of her girlfriends who had decided to meet us that night. She was having boy trouble and needed to blow off some steam, aka drink and smoke pot. Lacy asked if I minded her friend joining us, and I told her I didn't mind at all. I was so committed to my sobriety and my new life that even being around those things seemed harmless to me. Maybe I could even talk to the girl and give her some advice. Tell her that no amount of drugs or booze will fix the problem. It was worth a shot. I wanted to inspire as many people as I could on this trip.

Becky showed up and immediately ordered a strong drink. Lacy decided to have a drink as well. A Dirty Shirley: vodka, sprite and cherry juice. A drink we used to have together on many occasions. For a very brief moment, I heard that little dark voice creep in and say, "Wouldn't it be nice to have one with them? One isn't going to kill you."

I had been sober for over a year, and occasionally that voice would pop up again. As a recovering alcoholic and addict, that is something we must deal with often. But as a survivor, you have to keep reminding yourself that your life is so much better without those substances. You must remember some of the worst consequences you faced in your past, and tell yourself, "I am never going through that again." Every time.

So, once again, I bravely talked myself out of it, and the night continued. Becky was already an emotional wreck when she walked in, but as the drinks started flowing, she got progressively worse. She lit up a freshly rolled joint and started to cry. A boy she liked wanted nothing to do with her but continued to mess with her head. Flirting with her without making good on his advances.

Look, I've been through the same thing. Many times. I think we all have at some point in our lives. So I felt for her. Deeply. Then I gave her my advice. "Hey, it's gonna be okay. I promise. But you know what is not going to make it any better? Getting drunk and high. From my experience, when you use substances to try and fix the problems, more problems just appear. And most of the time, they are worse than the previous ones. Common math tells us that 1 + 1 = 2. In this case it's one bad emotional issue plus one bad night of drinking and drugging. The only answer possible to that equation is more bad. You are way too smart to do that kind of dumb math."

She tilted her head to the left and looked into my eyes. It was like a light went on. "You know what, you're right. I am smarter than that. Thank you," she said, wiping the tears from her eyes. The rest of the night was a little more lighthearted. Although the conversation occasionally deviated back to boys. Lacy's current on/off boyfriend and my old love interest, Liam, were mentioned a few times. I half expected him to show up that night. But he didn't. Thankfully.

When the night ended, I walked Lacy to her car, and she drove me back to the Airbnb. We said our goodbyes, and I headed straight for the bed. I had another busy day ahead of me on Sunday. I had made plans with Tim to record some video for a project he was working on for my book and, Jane and I would finally get our alone time after that. We hadn't had a good "J and K" day in far too long. I wondered if I would be strong enough to stay sober with the girl I used to party the hardest with. Only time would tell.

SUNDAY.
DAY FIVE.

IT WAS VERY EARLY on Sunday morning when I awoke. Tim had to work the shop that afternoon and suggested that we use the early part of the day for our project. The first stop would be Mel's Diner, where he would record an interview with me about my experience there.

When he came to visit me in NYC for my book release event, he had a brilliant idea to start filming interviews and readings at the places featured in the memoir. He took tons of photos when Clarke and I showed him around the homeless shelter and neighborhood we lived in when we first met. He also interviewed me at the 24-hour diner, where I had nursed a bagel and coffee for hours the first night I landed in New York because I had nowhere to sleep. Today he wanted to add to his compilation to get the LA parts of the book.

The LA segments he wanted to cover seemed like they would be the most emotional to recall. But I trusted Tim's vision and met him at the bakery that morning so we could get started.

Before I left, I put on a Johnny Cash t-shirt and a black faux leather jacket, similar to the ones I wore on my last night in Hollywood.

We jumped into his silver 4-door Toyota SUV and drove up the hill towards the restaurant. It was pretty surreal to be back in the passenger seat of his car again. A car that I had driven to drop off many important cakes and cupcakes in the past. Like the time I delivered a cake to the Playboy Mansion and was asked to stay and cut the cake for Oscar-winner Diablo Cody.

Tim had gotten really mad at me that night because I hadn't gone right back to the shop with his car and had decided to stay, drink and dance with the New Kids on the Block. Yeah, I had a one-on-one dance off with Joey from the group at the request of his wife. I ate personalized cupcakes with Hugh Hefner and the girls on the red velvet couch overlooking the grotto. And I definitely wasn't going to leave before I shared shots with Amanda Seyfried from Mean Girls. Tim was upset with me for a few days after that because he had to stay at the shop late into the night until I finally returned.

I wasn't always the greatest employee when it came to respect. Seemed like the only thing I respected back then was alcohol. I'm grateful for the familial relationship I had with Tim. If we hadn't been so close, I would have been fired many times over. But, he always saw the good in me. And now he was so proud of me. He was shouting my praise to every person who had not believed in me. He was a great surrogate father, and I was blessed to have him in my life.

His support had turned into inspiration and as we exited the car in the parking lot by Mel's, he started to film. "Let me get some shots of you walking up to the door. It might be a good transition clip."

Once he got the footage he needed, we headed in and grabbed a booth. It was the booth closest to the bar. The same booth where I had spent my last few moments in West Hollywood all those years before.

The waitress came over and handed us our menus. I ordered a coffee and Tim asked for a hot tea. He wasn't much of a coffee drinker. We looked through the food selections for a minute before he asked me if I was ready to start. The coffee and tea arrived before he could speak.

"So, Kaleb. Tell me about this place. How does it feel to be back?" he asked, pressing record on his phone's video app.

"It's a little strange. I am a completely different person than the last time I was here," I said, stirring Splenda into my coffee before continuing. "You know, people always say, 'Oh, he'll never change! People don't change!' and I always kind of thought that was true. But, here we are. Here I am: completely changed. It gives me hope for other people."

"What were you thinking about the last time you were here?" he asked, trying to take a sip of his tea and hold the phone steady simultaneously.

"Honestly, my thoughts were pretty dark. I was thinking about what a complete mess of a human being I was. How I had no one in my life that really cared for me," I said, looking at Tim, hoping not to offend him. Because he always cared. "It wasn't until after they put me in the back of that squad car that my thoughts turned desperate. Then I started seriously thinking about the ways I could end my life."

"And what stopped you from making that choice?" he asked, looking concerned, while zooming the lens closer to my face.

"I don't know. There was something inside of me that kept saying, 'This is not the end; you have more to give.' It sounded like my mother's voice."

"What do you think it was that got you to that point?" he asked. Tim knew the answer, but his interviewer skills were shining for the audience who didn't know my story.

"It was all of it. The eviction. The heartbreak. The lack of a job that I enjoyed. The betrayal. The drugs and the booze. The complete and utter loss of myself and my dreams." I said, stopping briefly for a moment to catch my breath and put my emotions in check. "I knew it was either kill myself or get the hell out of Los Angeles. I'm glad I went with the second option."

"I'm glad, too." Tim said as he pressed the record button again to stop the interview. "You really had me scared for a little while. I'm so proud of how far you've come."

That meant the world to me. Tim was the closest thing I had to a parent. When he told me he was proud, it was like the voices of my mother, father and grandmother were speaking through him. I was finally proud of myself.

We finished our food and recorded a few other questions and answers before heading to the car. Our next location was going to be even more emotional. Liam's old house. And the long stretch of road that led to it.

I swallowed my coffee and mentally prepared for the drive up the steep and windy hill that was Sunset Plaza Drive. The last time I traveled on that street, it was cold and dark. It would be interesting to see it again during the day. I guess it was sort of symbolic doing this interview during the day. My life had done a complete 180 from the darkness of before.

We got back into his silver SUV and drove. I didn't realize how far up the hill the house really was. I may have undersold the length of the walk in my first book. We were in a car this time, and it still took forever to get up there.

When we finally reached it, the flashbacks started to invade my mind.

My tear-soaked shirt and jacket. The sound of the door being slammed in my face by the man I had loved. The man I put so much faith into. The moments before that, though, when we sat so close to each other on his couch in his dark rock 'n' roll decorated living room. His music award trophies sitting on a shelf behind us while we sang. We really did make beautiful music together. All visions of a yesterday that were equally as nice as they were painful.

Tim tapped me on the shoulder to let me know he had found a parking spot near the house. I got out of the car carefully while holding a copy of my book. He was going to film me reading the part of the book where Liam decided to turn me away and at the same time break my heart. I knew it was going to be a tough read.

With the sun shining, surrounded by palm trees and overly priced houses, we recorded the segment on the dusty road. His house, sitting on a raised bit of land, served as the backdrop to the emotional retelling of the story. I opened my book to a page in the chapter entitled "The End" and began to speak the words I had written almost a year before.

When I got to the part about his car driving by with the music blaring, it was as if someone had been listening. At almost that exact moment, a vehicle like his drove by, interrupting the reading. I knew it wasn't him. He hadn't lived in that house for a while, but it was a crazy coincidence that made the video even better.

I picked up from where I left off and finished most of the chapter until I came to a powerful stopping point. It was strange. I didn't get as emotional as I thought I would. Maybe it was because I was over him? Or because I was hardened by all the struggles of my time in New York? Either way, I didn't cry. I didn't feel sad. I actually felt relieved. Like more weight was lifted from my shoulders. A peaceful feeling.

Once finished, I took one last look at his house and made a promise to myself that one day I would have my own house like that. I knew it would take a lot of work. But with my new outlook on life, and my sobriety, I knew that anything was possible.

Tim started the car and we drove back down the long, winding road. I recorded the descent and was shocked at how long the clip was upon playback. Once we returned to the cake shop, I received a text from Jane. She was ready for our "J and K" day and on her way to pick me up.

Jane arrived soon after her messages, and we shared an enormous hug the second we saw each other. We spent most of my book after-party sitting next to each other, but we didn't really get to talk alone. We had a lot to talk about. Like why we hadn't been in each other's lives that last year I was in LA. Where had she been?

Once in her car, our cigarettes lit, we headed east on Santa Monica Boulevard. We had discussed going to get red velvet pancakes from some organic restaurant she had heard about, but when we passed Barney's Beanery we knew we had to stop.

This bar was important to us because we had shared a few of our many adventures here. Like the night we got drunk, bought and ripped up some shirts from a guy selling them in a booth, and proceeded to dance inappropriately until we were kicked out. Another night here had led us back to my house, where we snorted cocaine while playing a drawing game with dry erase markers on my living room's hardwood floor. Then there was the night we decided to smoke pot at her place while her fiancé at the time was on tour. We somehow started a small fire on the floor, which she had to lie about afterwards to protect herself. And I'll never forget the time we went to a masquerade party at Hooters, and when we left we went to hail a cab, but instead a white stretch limo pulled over to pick us up. We drank the leftover liquor in the back, and I don't remember much else. I'm sure that was one of many nights that ended in a blackout.

Upon entering the bar, we half expected that they might remember us and tell us to leave. But, of course, they didn't. It had been many years since either of us had been to this place. It, like just about everything else, looked exactly the same. The only thing that had changed was us.

Jane looked very pretty that day. She always looks pretty, but at the moment she had a sort of glow. We sat at the table and ordered some food. She stuck to an all-vegan menu while I indulged on the greasy bar-type food. Hey! I was on vacation. We also ordered some drinks. I asked for a nonalcoholic beer and she requested a mimosa.

The conversation started out with general catching up but quickly moved to the more emotional stuff once the drinks arrived. She told me a harrowing tale of how dark her life had turned since we had last seen each other. She had experienced a few years of extreme heartache and pain similar to mine. She had found herself without a home at one point and told me she lived out of her car for a time.

I want to say that it shocked me, but even though she was beautiful, talented and intelligent, she was prone to the same addictions I had been struggling with. We held hands at one point and just sat there sharing a common condolence for each other.

"It seems like both our lives are on the up-and-up now," I spoke, breaking the momentary silence. I was grateful to be at a place in my life where my dearest friends from the past felt comfortable coming to me with these honest and painful memories.

"I'm really proud of you. It is amazing how far you have come since you quit drinking. It makes me think that I should give it a try, too," she said, pushing her almost empty glass of alcohol to the edge of the table.

"I think that is a good idea, Jane. I can say nothing negative about my sober experience. Was it hard at first? Yes. Is it still tempting sometimes? Yes. But, every day since I quit drinking and using drugs, my life has improved. And I will be here to support you," I responded, squeezing her hand a bit tighter.

"Thank you. That means the world to me," she said, trying to hold back a tear.

The waitress delivered the food to our table and looked at Jane's glass. "Would you like another mimosa?"

"No, thanks. How about one of those nonalcoholic beers!" she replied with a smile. The rest of brunch conversation was a little more lighthearted and the perfect start to a lovely day of reenacting some of our old shenanigans, minus the liquor and cocaine.

We paid our bill and headed to the bar patio for a cigarette. In order to get to the smoking area we had to walk by the bar and what we found there was very surprising. Tyler, another friend from the past I had shared many drunken and drugged-up evenings with.

Tyler was another one of those "straight guys" whom I had a little crush on when I was going to The State Room daily. He was a little older than I and sported dark, slicked-back hair, a strong, muscular upper body and some hipster style glasses. He and I were pretty close back then. Not as emotionally connected as Liam and me, but we had some semi-sexy moments back in the day. I think I even got him to kiss me a few times in exchange for some free cocaine.

As we passed by the bar, he noticed me first. It was like an explosion went off in the room when he recognized who I was. He bolted out of his seat, ran over to us, and picked me up in a very tight bear hug. It was definitely one of the sweetest welcome home reactions I had received so far. He was so emotional. I swear he cried a little.

"Oh my God! I can't believe you are actually here! It is so good to see you! You look so healthy, happy and gorgeous! Did you get a facelift?" he asked while still holding on to me tightly.

"Haha. No. I didn't get a facelift. This sobriety thing just seems to really be agreeing with me."

"It really does! So, tell me everything. I have been trying to keep up with you on Facebook, and it just seems like life is really treating you well these days. You definitely deserve it. You were always one of my favorite people," he said, finally letting me out of his loving death grip.

We sat and chatted with him and his lovely girlfriend for almost an hour. He was still into the drinking life but told me he had mostly quit using drugs. Which was a step in the right direction. Some people can handle the occasional drink and momentary high, but I don't think I am one of them. I mean, my self-control is very strong now, and I'm sure I could handle having just one drink, but why risk everything I have worked so hard for? It's a ridiculous thought to even consider. And it definitely would not be worth it. But, I am happy for the people that can handle it, the "normal" people. I've never been "normal," so why start now? Haha.

Tyler gave me another tight and lengthy hug before we left that afternoon. I hoped maybe seeing me being so successful after such struggle might rub off on him in some way. That's what my life was all about now, trying to inspire others. My goal would be achieved sooner than I thought, but not with Tyler, with someone even closer.

Jane and I got back in her car and headed back down Santa Monica towards the gay bars. We hit up my old favorite clubs, tipped a few go-go boys, and had nonalcoholic drinks the whole time. We also had a ton of fun. Just like the old days. We laughed and carried on like no time had passed.

Except now, our world wasn't focused on how many free drinks we could get, or where the drugs would come from; we were actually focusing on each other and the friendship we had both been missing dearly.

Before she dropped me off at the Airbnb that night, she told me how much fun she had and that she had "decided to give sobriety a shot."

"I know you'll be there to support me, Kaleb. Going out with you today and having nonalcoholic drinks made me realize that to be social and go out to the bars, I don't HAVE to drink. I guess it's just the kind of thing you do when you go out. Peer pressure. You're almost expected to have drinks and get drunk. I don't want that anymore," she said, holding my hand with her right hand while the other rested on the steering wheel.

"I've got your back, Jane. Now, and forever," I said, looking deep into my old best friend's eyes. She had a determination sparkling in those eyes, and I knew that if she put her mind to it, she'd be very successful on her sober journey.

I got out of the car feeling as if I was floating! One of the people I cared most about in the world made the best decision for her life, and I was her inspiration. I was so proud of her. And I was extra proud of myself. It further confirmed my new path in life, and I was beyond grateful that the Creator chose this road for me. But would she stay sober? Would I? Only time would tell. And tomorrow was another day.

MONDAY.
DAY SIX.

MONDAY MORNING! Another glorious day, and a new week, had begun in sunny Los Angeles. Today was a big day, because Cheri and I were going to go see the Conan O'Brien show. I was always a big fan of his and loved the beginning of each episode where someone in the front row got to pinch his nipple. It was a running gag that had been on the show for years, and I thought it would be great publicity if I was the one to do it today.

Before Cheri came to pick me up I headed over to the costume shop on Sunset Boulevard to grab a couple of things that might make the joke even better. I grabbed some fingerless faux leather gloves, fake earrings and a riding crop. I was gonna go for a full-on dominatrix-boy look, sure to make Conan giggle.

When I got to the hat aisle, I had a momentary flashback when I saw the top hats. I tried one on very similar to the one I had bought there a few years before. The hat I wore almost nightly when I went to the The State Room and partied my life away. The black top hat I wore the night I sang "Creep" at the Rainbow, hours before the rock star broke my heart. And that same hat I wore when I stepped off the train for the first time in New York City and saw the Diet Coke sign that read, "You moved to New York with the clothes on your back, the money in your pocket and your eye on the prize."

I didn't buy it. But I did take a few selfies in it to post on my Facebook. Almost as a tribute picture to the person I was before who was now, thankfully, dead. I whipped the hat off as soon as I was done snapping the pictures and left it, and those bad memories, on the shelf where they belonged.

With all my new costume supplies in hand, I purchased them and, even though I was carrying a bag full of stuff, walked out of the shop feeling a little lighter. It was like I had just left a dark part of me behind, and it felt great.

I waited for Cheri at The State Room and had a nonalcoholic beer while chatting with the staff. They were still giddy about the paparazzi photos of Justin Bieber holding my book. It was like I was finally the person I had wanted to be there all along. I was respected. And when I came in, they were happy to see me. It all felt like a dream, but luckily, it wasn't.

Cheri messaged me that she had arrived. I gave everyone a hug and raced out to the curb where she was waiting in her car. We shared a kiss on the cheek and then started driving toward the day's adventure.

What a drive! The scenery as we drove up Mulholland Drive towards the Hollywood hills was breathtaking. At one point we pulled over on a dirt-patch stretch of road and took photos of the Hollywood Sign that was shining before us. I don't think I had ever been that close to it. Or maybe I had been but didn't remember because of all the drugs and alcohol. It was a beautiful sight, and I was so happy to be seeing it for the first time with clear and sober eyes.

When we arrived at the studio parking lot, I started to put on my outfit for the day. All black, per usual, and the items I had bought earlier. I definitely looked like a funny, naughty dominatrix-boy. We got up to the front of the line and met with one of the production assistants. He really got a kick out of my outfit and my idea of being the person to pinch Conan's nipple. He said, "I'm gonna try to get you in the special seats in the front row. You guys look great. I think he will really get a good laugh from this."

Okay, cool. So maybe there was some magic still left in this trip. I mean, every day something kind of amazing happened, so why should today be any different? Cheri and I were both even more excited about the show with this possibility on the table. We sat under the giant Conan bobble-head statue and chatted while we waited.

I decided I would send Annette another message to see if she would answer. She did. But what she had to say was rather unexpected and quite scary. Her message read:

"Hi, Kaleb. I'm sorry I didn't get back to you sooner. Unfortunately, I wasn't feeling very well and had to be checked into the hospital. It looks like the cancer is back, but I think we caught it soon enough. I'm going to have to do more rounds of chemo and radiation. Hopefully, we can get rid of it for good this time. I might be in good enough shape for you to visit me on Wednesday if you can. Love, Annette."

Damn. It was hard to take the news in while sitting in the waiting area for the show. Here we were, about to do something fun, and Annette was laid up in some hospital bed feeling sick as a dog. It didn't seem fair. I was so sick of people I loved being affected by cancer. I wanted to scream but didn't.

I texted her back, letting her know I would come see her first thing Wednesday morning. She told me not to worry, as she was feeling better already and texted, *"Enjoy the show. Wish I was there!"* That put my mind at ease a little. She seemed in good spirits and that made me feel less guilty about enjoying the rest of my day. I couldn't wait to see her, though. Even if it was in a not-so-great situation.

I told Cheri what was going on, and she gave me a big hug. We sat there for a moment deep in thought, but before we knew it, the PA was calling for us to get on the VIP cart to take us to the studio. We shook off the sad vibes and perked up for what was sure to be an exciting TV adventure.

When we got into the studio we went to the seats up front that we had been instructed to sit in. A few minutes later, a woman came up to us and asked us to move. We told her that we had been assigned these seats by the gentleman outside, but she did not seem to care. I was a little upset. I had prepared for this moment so much! I had visualized it in my head. And it looked like it wasn't going to happen.

So I sat and pouted for a few minutes until the PA from outside came in to the studio. He walked up to us and had us move back down to the original seats. Great! So, it was going to happen. I was gonna be on TV, pinching Conan's nipple, in a hilarious little moment. A smile crept back into my face. But, lo and behold, the female PA came back and moved us back to the other seats. What the hell?!

Turns out she was the head PA in charge, and what she said was the final ruling. The other production assistant, who was so nice to us, came over and apologized. He told us that the people they replaced us with had been waiting in line for hours and the seats were rightfully theirs. He said, "It's too bad we won't get to see that bit! Maybe you can try it again one day." So, I was upset, but I understood.

The show was okay. Conan and Andy were funny, like always, but the guests weren't anyone we knew.

Either way, it was a fun experience to have with one of my best friends, and we enjoyed our time together. The real magic happened on the ride home.

Back down the hill, driving down Sunset towards Cheri's house, we came across a silver Bentley with a man driving who looked awfully familiar. "Oh, my god!" Cheri exclaimed. "I think that's David Beckham!!"

I had met David a few times back in my West Hollywood days. Mostly I would see him at the local Coffee Bean and Tea Leaf. One day, we even sat across from each other and chatted momentarily while waiting for our drinks. That day, I snapped a picture with him and didn't wash the shoulder for weeks where he had put his hand with his arm draped over me. (Just kidding, I washed it. But I thought about that moment for a while after it happened.)

I told Cheri to speed up a little so we could get a closer look. I thought maybe if I yelled out to him while we were at the red light, he might recognize me and say hello. Sure enough, when we pulled up, I yelled out, "Hey D! Big D! What's up?!"

He turned and looked over at us, gave us a big smile, and waved like a superstar. Cheri kept her cool for a minute, but as soon as he drove off, she squealed like a 12-year-old girl. Let's not kid ourselves, so did I. We giggled at how silly we both were acting but immediately told everyone we knew.

We decided to park the car at her apartment so she could show me her new place. It was a cute one-bedroom overlooking the Sunset Strip. A great location for a great girl. She gave me a tour of her humble abode and in the middle of the living room was her massage table. She was very serious about her new-found path in life, and that made me very happy for her. It was nice to see my friends making meaningful decisions that bettered their daily lives.

We freshened up and decided to head over to the Twisted Rainbow for an evening "drink." Nonalcoholic beverages, of course. We held hands as we walked down the street. There was a hum of happiness that seemed to float around us as we passed the other bars on the street. It was like we were on another pink cloud, and nothing bad could happen to us. That is, until we walked into the gates of our old stomping grounds and saw him.

There, on the back patio, was Liam. His back was facing us, but I knew immediately that it was the man who broke my heart. His same shaggy blonde hair, his same rock 'n' roll outfit, and his same voice that seemed to pierce through any of the other noise around us. I briefly saw his profile as he sat drinking, smoking and talking to some guy. I pulled Cheri by the arm and quickly ran to the dining area, inside the bar, so he wouldn't see us. I don't think I was quite ready to have "that moment" with him.

What was I going to say? How was I going to act? Would he even want to listen to what I had to say? And did I even want to have a conversation with him at all?

This is the man that single-handedly made me love again, then ripped my heart from my chest and sent me on the roller coaster ride that had been the toughest years of my life. But they had also been the most rewarding years, too. What would I even say? Would I cuss him out, or would I say "thank you" as I wrote about wanting to do in my book?

Cheri and I sat down inside the bar and ordered two nonalcoholic beers. She rubbed my back as I experienced a momentary hint of panic. My mind was racing, and I just couldn't decide what to do. I had been waiting for this moment for years. The tarot cards had predicted it would happen. So, why was I so shocked?

I thought about what a conversation with him now might do. What if it opened some old wounds or old emotional doors that I had closed already? What if he acted like nothing had happened? I was furious thinking about that. But there was a good chance that, even though he knew I had been gone, he might not realize how much he had hurt me. But, then again, maybe he did and he felt sorry.

While I was deciding what to do, a man came in from outside and sat a few stools down from us. The rock 'n' roll type, middle-aged, salt-and-pepper haired gentleman ordered a beer with an annoyed look on his face. He started a conversation with the bartender, and I can't say we were surprised by what we overheard.

"Ugh. I watched his damn dog for him. He still owes me for the last time. I even bought his plane ticket to the last gig. And does he pay me back?

No! Why do I keep helping this guy?" he asked the female bartender, as he took a big gulp from his glass bottle.

"I know, right? He asked me for a ride home a few weeks ago. He's lucky it was on my way to my house; otherwise, I would have said no. He's a mess," the bartender replied. They must have been talking about Liam.

Cheri and I had heard those stories many times, from many different people. In fact, we had told those stories of disdain in the past. When I heard he was going back on tour, I had sort of hoped that Liam had changed. That maybe somehow my choice to walk a grand new path had somehow manifested its way to his life. But, it didn't. Unfortunately, it sounded like he was the same old untrustworthy, alcoholic, drugged-up mess.

At that moment, I got up the courage to sign a copy of my book for him. I talked myself into going out there and giving it to him. I was going to face my fear and just see what happened. I just hoped that whatever occurred, that I would be strong enough not to fall for his tricks again. I didn't want to get sucked back into his world, or into his eyes.

I wrote a message that read:

"Liam. I don't really know what I can say, other than the words I have written in this book. Page 392. I wish you well. Please find yourself, and then maybe we can be friends again, one day. Stay Strong and Dream Big."

I don't know why I wrote that. Did I actually want to be friends with him again? Yes and No.

Not the way we had been before, though. Not a rehashing of the drinking buddies who came to love one another, but this time, I wanted to be a true friend. I wanted to be a good influence on him, as I had already been on Cheri and Jane. I guess I wanted to be the one that saved him.

I always saw the potential in him. And I thought that maybe, if he saw the new me, I could inspire him to sober up and really make it back into the spotlight so, he too, could inspire others. A lofty hope, I know. But that's what I did, now. I dreamed big.

I signed my name and got up to head out to the patio. The gentleman who had walked in earlier noticed Cheri and struck up a conversation. She knew him. She explained to me later that the guy was Liam's friend and helped him with his new tour.

"He left a little while ago," the guy said. "Fucking Liam! What a mess, that guy."

"Wait. He left?" I asked, hoping that it wasn't true. I had built up this whole moment and was ready to get it over with, and now I wouldn't get the chance. I walked out onto the back patio, holding the copy of my book I signed for him, and sure enough, he was gone.

By the time I got back inside, Liam's friend was gone, too. So, I sat back down at the bar with Cheri and kind of slumped over for minute. Damn, I had waited two and a half years, and twenty minutes, too late. But, maybe, that was not what the Creator wanted for me at that moment. Maybe, I wasn't supposed to talk with him just yet. I had learned to trust my path, and if it wasn't "supposed" to happen, then there was a divine reasoning behind it.

"Kaleb, if you want, I'll try and get the book to him. Let me hold onto it for you, and if the opportunity comes up, I'll make sure it gets to him," she said, putting her hand on my shoulder. She could tell I was a little irritated that I missed the chance to speak with him. But we both agreed that maybe it was for the best.

I still cared for him. I still cared for all my past friends and lovers. I even cared for my uncles in Texas who disowned me after my mother's death. I may not like some of those people for what they had done to me, but I would never wish harm upon them. Especially Liam. I hated the thought that one day I might get a call, or see a story on TMZ, saying that he had died of an overdose, and that I had not tried my hardest to help him.

Cheri and I finished our faux beers and thanked the staff for another interesting evening. This was another instance where if I had been drinking or using drugs, that a bender would have been unavoidable. But those thoughts didn't even cross my mind. Seeing Liam again, still in the throes of addiction, was a staunch reminder of why I was living the clean, sober life, now. I felt even more grateful for everything in that moment.

I called an Uber and headed back to the apartment where Mimi and Diana were sitting on the couch waiting to hear about the day's adventures. We spoke for a bit, and they gave me comforting words of advice. I really liked these two ladies and was thankful for this new-found friendship.

Later that evening, sitting on my bed, I let the day play back through my mind. Maybe I would see him again before I left, but maybe I wouldn't. Either way, I knew that my Higher Power had a plan for me, so I slept comfortably that night. I didn't think the trip could get more exciting than it had already been. But, boy was I wrong.

TUESDAY.
DAY SEVEN.

AFTER the previous night of drama, a fresh start in the morning was very welcomed. I made a few plans with more people I had not seen in what felt like decades. First up for the day was a trip to the cake shop to tell Tim and crew about the evening before and maybe to help out a little. It had been some time since I had frosted a cupcake!

When I opened my bedroom door, I greeted the girls as they began their morning workout and headed to the patio to write my daily Facebook post. I made mention of the previous night's encounter but didn't elaborate much. I wasn't trying to drum up those emotions first thing in the morning.

After the obligatory morning cigarette and blog entry, I headed to the cake shop. Each day, walking down that stretch of road again, I remembered how beautiful the city was and why I was so attracted to it in the first place. The ripped, shirtless, man jogging by me didn't hurt my eyes, either. I felt so lucky to be back, and for that I had to thank Tim.

Tim was already manning the phones and scribbling out an order when I walked in. The bakery was busier than ever, and everyone was diligently working away. The atmosphere was filled with new life. The bustle seemed different from the memories I had of the place. It was busy back then, but there was always a dark cloud hanging over it all. Maybe that dark cloud back then was me. Today, there was a light in the building. Hopefully now, that was me, too.

Tim hung up the phone and said a brief hello before the phone started ringing again. I walked into the kitchen and gave everyone a hug. Being greeted with smiles was another amazing side effect of my new life. Even Marc, who had seen me at my worst, was smiling and proud of me. And even though there were a bunch of new faces, it felt like the cake family was finally back together.

I decided I wanted to try my hand at decorating some cupcakes again and had Angie film the quick process for my Facebook page. I placed the moist chocolate cupcakes onto the large wooden table. The table and most of the equipment was older than I was, and I loved the history of it all. I scooped some rich chocolate frosting into a piping bag and began to ice the cupcakes. It came back to me like second nature. A quick couple of clockwise squeezes of the bag, and the frosting was perfect. Then I added a few chocolate sprinkles, and I was done! As I put them into the display case, I grabbed a red velvet for myself and devoured it in seconds. Red velvet was always my favorite.

Before I left the bakery, I grabbed two copies of my book. I had made a joke the last time I left about possibly seeing a celebrity to give a book to, and look what happened. I was definitely not going to be unprepared. I couldn't get the message in the tarot cards out of my head, and this was Hollywood --there was magic in the air. Anything could, and most likely would, happen.

Tim winked from his seat by the front desk, the phone still glued to his ear, when he saw me put the books into my bag. I waved goodbye quietly, as not to interrupt his call, and headed out the door. I had made a lunch date with Wendy, and the time was nearing.

We decided to meet at the Twisted Rainbow that afternoon. They did make good food, but maybe I was hoping to run into Liam again. I still felt slightly annoyed that I hadn't gotten my moment with him the way I had pictured it. Wendy agreed, unaware of my reasoning for choosing that place. I grabbed an Uber and headed up the block.

Daytime on the Sunset Strip was probably a rare sight for most Angelenos, but for me, it was an old everyday occurrence. It was during the day when Liam and I got close at the bars and actually had some semi-private time together. I figured since it appeared he hadn't changed much, that he might still be taking part in an afternoon drinking routine.

I arrived at the bar first. Liam wasn't there, but Cynthia was, and she pulled out a nonalcoholic beer before I even sat down. "It's still a little strange that this is your drink, now. But, I'm proud of you, Kaleb," she said, handing the bottle to me across the old oak bar. I poured it into the accompanying frosty glass and patiently awaited my dear French pastry chef friend.

Wendy arrived within minutes and looked as lovely as ever. We sat outside on the patio and ordered a round of drinks. Cynthia brought us the menus and gave an extra wipe to the table, to assure its cleanliness after another crazy night. The table that just happened to be the one Liam was sitting at. Call me crazy, but I kind of wanted him to walk in right then, so I could get everything off my chest that had been festering for years. I felt I deserved that kind of closure, at the very least.

He didn't make an appearance. But Wendy and I still had a lovely time catching up. She was working at a new place where she was top dog. She told me about loving her new position but said the hours were sometimes excruciating. She had a sexy new Porsche and a sexy new man. She was head over heels, and it was so nice to see her happy after all this time.

Wendy and I hadn't connected right away, back when I was living at the restaurant for a few weeks. I think it took her a little time to trust me the way

Leah had seemed to do almost immediately. But Wendy was the one who came through for me with my bag of clothes and laptop when I decided to leave so abruptly. And it was Wendy I called when I was in the shelters to ask for advice and tell her of my life wins. She became a true friend, and I was beyond grateful to have her in my life.

We finished our meal, and she asked, "So what are your plans for the rest of the time you are here? Are you gonna sing here at the Rainbow?"

Wait. What a brilliant idea! Why hadn't that crossed my mind? Performing at the same place, on another Wednesday night before leaving LA, would be quite the full circle moment.

"Wendy! That is a great idea, but I don't even know if they are still doing the jam nights. And I wouldn't know who to contact," I said, pursing my lips in deep thought.

"Ask around! If anyone can make it happen, it's you, Kaleb!"

Well, I definitely appreciated the vote of confidence pouring from my friend's mouth. Hopefully, she was right.

She pulled her keys from her purse and stood up from the bar-height table. I got off my bar stool and grabbed her for another long, heartfelt hug. We had both come such a long way in a relatively short amount of time. Our lives had both changed for the better. Not that hers was bad before, but she seemed much happier and more fulfilled. Which is all one can really ask for in life, right?

She hurried out through the gate to her car, off to a meeting at the new restaurant. I sat back down at the table and continued to ponder how I could make the performance happen. As I took another sip of my frosty nonalcoholic beer, the owner and his son walked in. Talk about a blast from the past!

Like the previous meetings with old friends and acquaintances, they were shocked at my changes, too. We all spoke for a little while, and I filled them in on the stories from the past few years. When I pulled out a copy of my book, the owner immediately asked to see it.

I told him that I mentioned the bar in my writing and how thankful I was for the opportunity the place had given me to express my talents and my uniqueness, even when I was a mess. He smiled and began to browse through the pages. I decided to sign and leave a copy with him. As I wrote the message I asked, "Do you know if the female drummer is still the host of the jam nights? Are you still even doing them?"

"Thanks for the book, I'm definitely interested in reading it. And yeah, she is still hosting," he said, taking the book with pride. That meant a lot to me; to see a little bit a of pride on this man's face. This guy partied with most of the biggest names in rock 'n' roll, watched unknown bands perform on his stage before they became big stars, and was there to cheer me on the last night I was in LA, singing "Creep" on his stage. So, to get his approval was a huge honor.

He grabbed his drink and took my book to his office. Our little shared moment inspired me to jump up to the bar and ask Cynthia if she knew how to contact the lady drummer, whose name I had forgotten. Within minutes, she found me the Facebook page for the event and the talented percussionist, Jamie. I immediately sent a message asking if it was possible for me to perform the following night.

I didn't hear back from her right away, but I did get a text message while I waited. It was from my friend, Joey. A good looking, Spanish, masculine, helicopter-company-owning, former cop who was a self-proclaimed bisexual (but I had only ever seen him date guys). We had been friends for many years and had a lot of history. I always felt a little bit of sexual tension with him. But, most of the times we were out together, I was a drunken mess, which deterred attraction from a lot of people.

In his message he asked if I was free to meet for dinner and some one-on-one time. He had come to the book signing and after-party where I sat on his lap for a while, playfully flirting. I wondered if maybe he had taken a liking to the new version of me and was planning to make his move tonight. The way my week had been going, one never knew!

I agreed, and we decided to meet at The Abbey later in the evening. So, with time to kill, I decided to pay my tab and head down to Melrose Avenue to see if I could run into my old drag queen boss, Cosmo, from the first year I lived in LA. He had been sober for quite some time, and I knew he would be very proud of all my accomplishments through sobriety.

I took an Uber down to the most fashionable street in town and began to look for my old mentor. I became distracted by the funky shops and came across an amazing t-shirt that I had to buy. It was like a sign from the Creator. The dark grey shirt had what looked like a postcard of the Hollywood Sign high above a palm tree-lined street. But upon closer inspection, I noticed that the sign didn't spell out Hollywood, it formed the words New York City.

It was perfect. It was like a strange symbol for my life at that moment. New York had been where my dreams had come true, a twist of fate, because I had fully expected to make it happen in Hollywood, all those years ago. I bought it and changed into it before I left. I quickly snapped a selfie in my black reflective lens Ray Bans, pointing to the sign and posted it to my Facebook. *"Where the magic really happens."*

I couldn't find Cosmo anywhere but noticed he had purchased and opened another new, funky boutique. The employees inside told me he was out gathering new apparel for the store, and they would gladly take a message for me. I wrote him a sweet note and left my phone number and the address to my book's website. *"Thanks for being you and accepting me for me,"* I wrote at the end of the note. I left feeling happy for him since he had been through a rough couple of years, as well. But it looked like he had turned everything around and was thriving. My heart felt filled and relieved for my old friend.

Joey texted me that he was on his way to West Hollywood, so I called for another car and headed that way, too. I was excited to share some alone time with my old buddy and see what the evening had in store for us. I was in for a shock when another bit of in unexpected magic occurred.

We both arrived at the place around the same time and grabbed some seats at the patio bar. We perused through the menu and ordered some drinks. I had a nonalcoholic Mojito, and he had a real one. We chatted for a bit, sitting awfully close to each other. I flirted with him a little, but mostly in a playful way. Even though my body was completely shaven, and I was beyond ready to be with someone again, I felt like it was better to just leave the friendship in the good place it was at and not push the issue. We ordered food and began to converse about the changes in our lives.

A few minutes passed and a very tall African-American gentleman walked in and pulled up the chair next to us. He looked very familiar. He was sporting some hot shades, a blue ball cap and some Adidas pants and shirt. He looked over at me, and then I recognized him almost instantly. It was none other than one of the most famous former basketball players in the world, who most recently made world headlines for hanging out with one of the world's most notorious dictators. (I promised him if I ever wrote about the moment that follows, I wouldn't use his name. So, I am keeping my word.)

He asked me if I had a light for his big, fancy cigar. I obliged and said, "Hey, I think we've met. Were you at the Oscar party here a few years ago?!"

"Oh yeah, yeah. I always come out to support a good cause. I thought you looked familiar. Thanks for the light," he said as he walked over to talk to the table of people behind us.

Joey started to freak out. He couldn't believe he had just met a famous celebrity and was even more shocked that I already knew him. He said, "Before we leave, I have to give him my card! I bet he could use my copter services."

We finished eating, and when Joey got up to give the famous basketball player his card, I decided maybe I would give him a book, too. It had been reported that he, too, had his issues with drugs in the past, so I thought maybe he could possibly connect with my story and offer me some advice on how to get it out to the public a little more efficiently.

We walked up to the table and I politely got his attention. Joey handed him his card, and they talked for a moment. When they finished, I asked, "Would it be okay if I gave you a copy of my book?"

"Hmmm. I'll tell you what, if you can read us one paragraph that really gets me, I'll take it. And I'll read it," he said, looking at the cover suspiciously.

I opened my book up to page 327 and read him the paragraph about the moments leading up to and how I finally decided I had to quit drinking and using drugs. The table went silent for a minute. And then he looked up at me.

"Man, that was good. That was real. I felt you, man. Good stuff. I'll take it. You gonna sign it for me?"

As I signed it, the people at the table started to share their stories with me. Stories of drug abuse, heartbreak and forgotten dreams. We all had a powerful conversation that seemed to last for hours. We were so open and so understanding of one another. It was truly a beautiful meeting that I will cherish forever.

Before I left, I told them how my story ended up. The TV shows, the movies, the book and the lives I had already been affecting. One of the girls took me to the side and hugged me tightly as she shed a tear.

"I'm so glad you came up to our table tonight. You truly inspired me. I'm gonna do some of things I have been holding off on. Thank you. Thank you so much."

"You are so welcome, darling. I'm glad this happened, too. It was a really magical moment. Thank you for being so open," I said, giving her an extra squeeze before letting go.

We all took a group photo together, and the famous basketball star held my book in his hand. I thanked everyone again for a lovely time, and Joey and I exited feeling amazing. The magic had found me again. I couldn't have been prouder that evening. I had found my divine path and was fully committed to it, and I was making a difference by just being me. It was one of those moments that I silently gave gratitude to the Powers That Be for the blessings they had bestowed on me since the day I quit drinking and using drugs.

Joey dropped me off at the apartment, and again I hit the bed that night with a feeling of the best kind of exhaustion ever. But before I fell asleep I got a message from my drummer friend.

"Hey! Yes, we still do jam nights! I'd love it if you came and sang a song with us. I can get you a slot around 10 or 11 p.m. See you tomorrow! So happy to see all the amazing progress you've made since I last saw you. - Jamie"

I quickly texted back that I was confirmed for the next day and that I was beyond excited.

It looks like the full circle moment I hoped for would in fact come to fruition. Was it manifested or was it magic?

Wednesday was going to be a busy day. First thing in the morning I was going to see Annette in the hospital. I hoped I would be strong enough to handle whatever I might see. Thoughts of my mother lying in her hospital bed, attached to wires and a breathing tube, crept into my head. It scared me a little, but I knew Annette was not that bad off. So I fell asleep with a bit of comfort and hopes for another magical day tomorrow.

WEDNESDAY.
DAY EIGHT.
FULL CIRCLE.

THIS MORNING, waking up was not particularly exciting. I mean, it was a beautiful day; the sun was shining and the birds were singing, but my first task for the day was to go see one of my best friends in the hospital. Not something you just jump for joy to do, but I was anticipating seeing her again.

I got up and went about my daily routine. The only thing that kept going through my mind were pictures of the last day I saw my mother in the hospital and all the regrets I had from back then. If only I had known that those would be the last months my mother had to live, I would have been by her bedside every day. But, I was a senior in high school, and she made sure that I focused on my studies.

I wholeheartedly believed she was going to make it through. She was an award-winning nurse; she knew a lot of the hospital staff treating her, and she was as tough as nails. She had beat so many other crazy sicknesses and medical traumas throughout her life, that this seemed like another surefire win. I remember watching her go from my mother, to a sickly, bald, bloated human being, and that's a picture that is hard to get out of my head. But the other memories are so much stronger.

One of my favorite memories with her was when she let me volunteer at the hospice she managed. She was the head nurse and by far the most loved and respected. Those summers at the facility taught me how to face death and realize that it is something natural that we can't escape. I bathed some of the patients with her and came to love them and their families. When they died, I learned about my personal strength. I know now that those summers were to prepare me for the moment when I had to make the decision to no longer let my mother suffer and pull the plug when the doctor advised.

Standing there with my family, at 18 years old, holding hands and being the one to pray out loud over her dying body while everyone else cried, I grasped the greatness of the Universe. I didn't know it at the moment, but maybe, when she opened her eyes to look at me for the last time, she was transferring her strength to me. I don't know where I would be right now had she lived. It's nice to think about, but I know, everything happens for a reason. And I am grateful for who

I am today; the passionate life I am leading, and that her voice has been with me to reassure and encourage me every step of the way.

I finished dusting the bronzer on my face when I got a text from Annette asking what time I was coming. I was glad to see she was up and feeling ready for company. It immediately put my mind at ease and made the scary thoughts disappear. The beauty of the day was now something I could admire with the positive outlook that suddenly washed back over me.

I requested a car and headed to the hospital in Burbank.

Thirty or so minutes later, after driving up and down the winding hills of Hollywood, I arrived at the medical center. Walking into the door, to the familiar sights of a busy hospital, reminded me of the year before when I had to visit another friend in a cancer ward. That time, though, it was Clarke, and it was in New York City. The "why me?" voice started to play in my head briefly. I was tired of having to go through this with people I cared deeply about. I know it pales in comparison to the amount of emotional stress they dealt with, but it still felt like a bad deal, either way.

I didn't know what to expect when I entered the room. I definitely didn't want to go in empty handed, so I stopped by the gift shop. I looked around for a few minutes, taking in all the different trinkets and displays of flowers. Nothing seemed perfect enough for Annette. I didn't want to get her some flowers that would just die in a few days. That didn't ever seem like a good message to send to someone in the hospital. I had almost given up when I got to the register. Then I saw the cutest little bear.

The little teddy was in a skeleton costume for Halloween, and I took it to mean that it was trying to show sickness that it was not so scary. Not as scary as a sweet little bear in a skeleton costume. Or maybe it was trying to show it had strong bones underneath the fluffy exterior and that Annette was strong under it all, too. It may seem like I was trying to stretch the different meanings of the stuffed animal, but I wanted it to have a lasting message. It is said that there is power within special objects given with love. So, if there was any magic left in this trip, I hoped that it would all turn into healing waves and radiate through this bear to my dear friend.

The walk down the long, white, sterile hallway gave me time to put on my happy face. She had warned me that she might not look like herself, but I was pleasantly surprised when I entered the room to see that same, happy German smile I had been missing. She did look a little thinner and was donning a wig, but what did I expect? She was fighting a terrible disease. Her natural blonde locks were replaced by a wig made of very high quality faux strands of blonde hair. Something Sarah Summers would definitely wear. She looked really good, though, especially for being hospitalized a few days prior.

Her daughter was there, too. I had missed both of their faces so much. She ran up to me and gave me the biggest hug she could. I didn't look like the person they remembered, either. The first words out of Annette's mouth were, "Wow! You look so healthy! So handsome! Happy!" It was the same chorus the choir of well-wishers in West Hollywood had been singing, but from her, as when Tim said it, it meant a little more. She, too, had seen me at some of my worst moments. But now I got to be there for her when she needed me.

My first order of business was to lighten the mood. "You have to tell me where you got your hair! It's fabulous! Sarah could totally rock those locks," I said, fluffing my invisible hair while making a sultry face.

They both started to giggle, and I felt some of the weight of the room lift. "Laughter is the best form of medicine," my friends, the proverbial THEY, always say. So, I did what I do best and told jokes in hopes that I could make them both feel a little better. And it seemed as if it might have worked a little when Annette asked for some real food. Her daughter, Carly, and I headed down to the cafeteria to see what we could find.

I was kind of nervous about that walk and elevator ride. I had once been that child whose mother was sick with cancer. I understood her in a way that other people couldn't, because I had been there. I had been so confident that my mother would live, and I was quietly devastated when she passed, even though I kept strong for my family's sake. I wanted to say the right thing to Carly. I wanted to be the voice that I wish I had back then. So I tried my best to reassure her that no matter what happened, she would be okay.

I had high hopes for Annette, too. This wasn't her first bout with this particular kind of cancer, but God willing, it would be her last. Clarke beat his cancer; Annette would, too. I prayed silently as we entered the elevator and slowly made our way down to the eatery.

Carly was a beautiful, strong young lady, and she was very talented, too. We connected on our shared love for acting and entertainment. She was becoming something of a YouTube personality and already had done some roles on TV and film. We chatted about acting while we picked up some food for ourselves and a hamburger for Annette.

I gave her a big hug on the ride back up to the third floor and told her that I would be there for her whenever she needed me. "I'm always a phone call, a text, or a plane ride away." She smiled, and I felt our connection grow stronger in that moment. We got back to the room with food in hand and Annette's face lit up with joy.

"It truly is so good to see you, Kaleb. After all this time talking on the phone and really worrying about you, I'm glad you are here. You know you scared me, but I knew you would make it through it. Okay, enough mushy talk. Give me that hamburger," she said, stretching out her arms, still attached to wires, and grasping in the air in a comedic way.

We all enjoyed our lunch together, and I started to feel a little more confident that Annette really would be okay. Before I left, I gave them both the biggest, most heartfelt hugs I could muster. I didn't know the next time I would see them again, but

I knew it wouldn't take me two and a half years to get back this time. It was an emotional ending to the morning visit, but there were no tears shed. Because we all knew it wasn't our last goodbye. It was more of a "see you soon!"

The car ride back to the apartment was somber and a tad bittersweet. This was my last full day in Los Angeles, and I made sure to cram it full of things that were sure to be memorable. I did make a little time for some very much needed relaxation by the pool. I couldn't quite come to LA in the summer and miss an opportunity to take a dip and decompress. I had spent an hour using Nair and shaving before I left New York, so I might as well get some use out of my hairless and svelte, sun-deprived body. I had also purchased a sexy little WeHo style swimsuit when I was out with Joey the day before, and it would be a shame not to show it off. Plus, the man of my dreams might just happen to be sitting by the pool today. Haha. "Dream big," I always say.

I got back to the apartment, squeezed into my figure-hugging shorts, grabbed my headphones and headed to the pool. It seemed like the perfect moment to listen to the newly purchased Britney Spears album I had downloaded to my phone. It still tickled me to think how perfect it was that her album release just happened concurrently on the same day as my big book signing. I wondered if the songs on this album would parallel my life as much as the last ones had.

There was no one by the pool when I got there. So, I guess I wouldn't be finding Prince Charming by the water, but I would finally have some time to myself to actually let everything that had happened up until now, finally sink in. It had been a big week. Ridiculously big! Magical.

Lying there with the sun beating down on my freshly shaved body, I put my headphones on, started the music, and closed my eyes. A smile slowly stretched across my face without even trying. As the first song began to play, I felt like I was floating again. I thought about how grateful I was at that very moment. It was like I was in paradise when my eyes were closed, and when I opened them again, the visions were real. I wasn't dreaming.

The Universe had provided me with so many gifts and, for once, I finally felt deserving of it all. And there is nothing wrong with that. If the things that happened that week, and the amazing months before, had happened when I was drinking and using drugs, I definitely would have felt undeserving. Actually, I probably wouldn't have recognized the magnitude of it at all, and I definitely wouldn't have been appreciative or grateful.

When the album reached its last track, I was surprised to hear that it was completely in French! My New York life was surrounded by my French job and the constant French chatter (most of which I didn't understand) from my spiritually adoptive French mother and the staff. It just made strange sense that Britney would put a song in the language I had become accustomed to hearing. It made me wonder what sort of "Frenchness" was going on in Ms. Spears' life that led her to record that song. I just took it as another sign that everything was exactly as it was supposed to be in the world, and I just continued to smile.

I swam a couple of laps in the warm water before I looked at the time and realized I had to get ready to meet up with Cheri so we could go to the Chamber of Commerce mixer. I was excited to see all of my business cohorts again, and more importantly, show them the new me. Long gone were the days when I would go to the monthly mixers to drink all the free booze, flirt with the cute membership guy, and pretend to network. Today, it would be all about promoting my book and seeing people I respected and missed dearly.

I put on my cutest business casual look and headed up to Sunset Boulevard to meet with Cheri. We stopped by The State Room for a quick minute to see Ray and have a nonalcoholic beer. She was definitely still on the sober train, and I couldn't have been happier. Now, if only I could be that good of an influence on everyone, I'd have it made!

While we chatted, I got a text message from Jane letting me know that she would be meeting us at the Rainbow later to watch my performance. She also let me know she was still sober, *"3 days!"* and made it her plan to stay that way. I guess I really was having a positive effect on the people I cared about and again, I felt so grateful for the opportunity to do so.

We walked a few blocks over to where the mixer was being held. It was at a newly-constructed Spanish restaurant, doors down from Book Soup.

It was very nicely decorated and when we walked in, I started seeing familiar faces almost instantly. It was like a ghost had just walked into the room. People reacted in the same general tone that I had encountered the whole week. It was beautiful. And two people made me especially happy when I saw them.

Nadia was a fiery red-head with a thick, French-sounding accent and a fierce personality. She was an older woman, but you couldn't tell by meeting her. She was always so full of energy, and she never lacked support for me. Even when I was struggling, I could always count on Nadia for sound advice and a full-hearted hug every time I saw her.

She was a pioneer in the West Hollywood community and started an amazing organization called PAWS LA, which helped people with chronic illnesses take care of their pets when they couldn't afford to, or weren't physically able. She supported my effort to host a puppy fashion show to benefit her charity when I was working at the cake shop and had created a line of fancy fresh-baked pet treats. That event was a big success, and it was one of the few moments where I hadn't let my love of booze get in the way of something wonderful. Seeing her again on this day was long awaited.

When she recognized me, she ran up to me and planted one of her signature hugs tightly on me. You can probably guess the first words out of her mouth. "Oh my! You look so healthy, so happy, so handsome," she said, twirling me around to get the full view.

"Thank you, Nadia. You look lovely as always. Do you remember my friend, Cheri?"

"Of course! Good to see you, sweetie!!" she said, pulling in Cheri for a warm hug, too.

The ladies started talking about their shared love and knowledge of Reiki healing. The networking was happening already! While they chatted, I looked around the room and spotted another sorely missed face. It was that of my friend, Teri. She had been a customer of Hollywood Cakes and a person I would always hang out with at the mixers.

Teri was a light brown-haired, shorter lady with glasses and a kind face. She was a career coach and was leading the way by helping people in the city prepare for jobs specifically fit for them. A real positive life force in the world. When she saw me, she started to tear up a little.

We shared a big hug, and I told her my story of the last few years. When she heard that I had been in town for the book signing, she almost lost it. "Oh my gosh! I need a copy of your book! Sorry I didn't know about the event. Can I get one over there now? You'll have to personalize it for me!" she said, her glasses almost falling off her sweet face as she spoke excitedly.

"Haha. Yes, they have a few copies left over there. If you want to run a few doors down and pick one up, I'll be here, and gladly sign it for you. You were always one of my favorite people in this town. It's really good to see you again," I said, getting a little emotional as I hugged her tightly. I had sort of forgotten how many great people I had in my life in West Hollywood. How did I let one bad apple, and a few really crappy moments, almost ruin all those lovely memories? I was pleased that I was finally able to appreciate the great people in my life with these sober eyes.

While she went to the book store, I sat down with Cheri at the bar, and we both politely waved away the servers offering free drinks as they passed us. Having a sober bestie by my side was nice to experience. Not that I really cared if people around me drank or not, but it made the evening more enjoyable knowing that I had someone on my same level. It put my mind at ease not having to worry about dealing with a drunk person when the evening wore down. Oh, how times had changed. I understood more and more what my friends in the past had to deal with, and I appreciated them each even more now.

Teri came back; I signed the book, and we shared some laughs. The President of the Chamber made her speech towards the end of the event and gave a little nod and mention to me. She and I shared a nice hug before Cheri and I left. I walked out feeling like a million bucks. It's like I had an imaginary list of redemption and I was dutifully checking off each box.

Face Fears.

Check.

Show doubters and disbelievers the new you.

Check.

Make amends when necessary.

Check.

Make an impact on the people closest to you.
Check!
Perform the song that meant so much to you in the last few years at the place you originally sang it.
Almost check.

The last thing on the list was now just a few hours away. I went back to the Airbnb with Cheri and got dressed in the new outfit I had purchased just a few days before. Tight, black leathery-looking jeans, my black cowboy boots, a black faux-leather jacket, and a new faded-looking Johnny Cash t-shirt. All the items were eerily, and purposefully, similar to the ones I had worn the last time I was on that famous rock 'n' roll stage. The perfect outfit for the perfect ending to this magical trip.

Cheri and I headed to the Twisted Rainbow after stopping by her house so she could put on something a little less business causal, as well. Jane decided to meet up with us a little earlier at the bar for some nonalcoholic beer and conversation. The talk that we had really made me wish I could stay longer.

Sitting at a table on the patio, close to the front gate, the topic of the evening was sobriety. It was heartwarming to hear two of my besties, whom I had drunk tons of booze and used many drugs with, speak so hopefully of their plans to stay sober.

"It's only been a few days, but I'm feeling better already, more motivated," said Jane, smiling from ear to ear. "I'm so glad you introduced me to the idea of nonalcoholic beer and mocktails. I thought going out meant I had to drink. It's just kind of expected. But I've seen the way you are, and you haven't given up going out or being social."

"Exactly. I found a way to make going out still enjoyable. And look, we are actors, so a fake beer is just like a prop in a scene challenge for us. And maybe, it sort of has a placebo effect," I said, taking a swig from the bottle. "But luckily, there are no blackouts, no drunkenness and no hangovers!"

"Look at the three of us. Sober as Gophers!" Cheri exclaimed, raising her bottle to cheers us.

"Haha. Totes MY goats," I replied, knowing I had said the term wrong in order to get a laugh.

We clinked our faux beers and giggled. The night was young, and I was so happy to be with these two amazing girls. Lacy texted me and said she wouldn't be able to make it, but it was a quick call from Tim that really surprised me. He decided he wanted to come out to support me and watch me sing. Whoa! Tim, out at a rock 'n' roll bar, late into the evening? It was shocking! This is the man who worked 12-hour days at the cake shop and, back in the day, I could barely get to have dinner with me after the shop closed. It seemed like some things actually had changed when I was in New York, and they were welcomed improvements on the past.

We walked upstairs when the doors finally opened and I met with my spunky blonde drummer friend, Jaime, to discuss when I would be singing.

She put me on the list for 10 p.m. and started asking her band mates if they knew the music to "Creep." She received a few side to side head shakes from the guys around her. Wait? They didn't know how to play "Creep?" Damn it! Could it be possible that my big "full-circle moment" dream would not actually come to fruition?

I got a little worried, but she told me, "It is a jam night, so don't worry. I'm sure somebody who knows the guitar part to your song will show up." I sure hope she was right. I mean, it really didn't matter in the grand scheme of things if I performed the song that night or not. I had already accomplished so many awesome triumphs during my trip, but having that moment would have just been the storybook ending to a magical adventure. I didn't give up hope, but I didn't let it bother me too much, either.

Tim met up with us a little later that evening after delivering a few cakes to the big nightclub account I helped set up back in 2008 when the economy was a mess. I was happy the cake shop was still doing so well and that he seemed to be happier than ever before. He was a little more adventurous, too! As we all sat across from each other at an old wooden table in the upstairs bar, I felt an immense amount of love and pride flowing in my direction. Three of the most important people in my life were by my side for my last night in Hollywood. A stark contrast to the loneliness I experienced sitting at that same table just two and a half years earlier.

Tim filmed a little video of me and the two girls goofing off and sharing a silly kiss, trying to vamp it up for the camera. I guess I really did beguile women! (That was a big word Tim had used in the description on the back of my first book, and I didn't quite know what it meant back then. Haha.) While we chatted and danced around in our chairs, a few more regulars I had known in the past showed up. Another 30 minutes flew by and I was still holding out a shred of hope that someone who knew how to play the song would make an appearance. Thankfully, I didn't have to wait too long.

In the middle of taking a swig of my beverage, Jaime waved at me to get my attention. A guitar player who knew "Creep" had just made his way to the stage. She held up her open hand, fingers stretched out, to let me know I would be going on in 5 minutes. Wow. At 11 p.m., when I had almost given up, and Tim was getting ready to leave, it was now just minutes away from my full-circle moment. I got a little nervous, and for the briefest of seconds, that little voice in my head said, "Wouldn't a shot of fireball be amazing right now? It would really calm these nerves."

Good try, you evil bastard! Yes, in the past, a shot, or 5, would have been amazing, but it also would have led to slurred sung words and missed beats. And more than likely, an unthinkable plethora of disastrous events would follow. I resisted yet again, but I wondered, would that voice ever go away for good? Even after a year of sobriety, it still popped up sometimes and when talking to sober people, who have many years under their belt, they tell me it gets easier, but it is always there. You just have to stay strong.

One minute to showtime. Cheri and Jane had their phones ready to record, and Tim would be going live on Facebook from my phone. I stood up, brushed the nerves off, and headed to the stage. That same legendary spot where many rock legends had made their mark over the years. The lights were down low, a smoky haze filled the room, and the mic stand seemed to call my name in its imaginary, deep, raspy voice.

I place my hand upon the microphone as the guitar began to play. The melody was eerie in the most familiar and beautiful way. With passion in my eyes, I looked up into the lens of my iPhone's camera and began to sing the words I had sung at some of the biggest milestones in the last few years of my life. This night, the words meant so much more. And when I got to the last few strings of lyrics, I changed them up, as I always did, to speak what was in my heart.

"I'm a creep. You're a weirdo. What the hell are we doing here? It's 'cause we belong here. You know I belong here...."

It was true. We are all misunderstood; we are all different; we are all creeps and weirdos, but we all belong. And on this night, I truly felt as if I belonged on that stage. I had fought tooth and nail to get back to Los Angeles, back to a life I was proud of, and to a place where I felt wanted and accepted. Surrounded by my dear friends whom I considered family, I finally felt that magical release I had been waiting for. It was done. The performance, the redemption, the amends and, unfortunately, the trip.

When the applause rang out, and I looked at my watch, I realized it was late, and this was really my last night in LA. But this time, I would get to say my proper goodbyes, and I wasn't running away from anything. It was a bittersweet thought, but I knew I had to do it. I wanted to leave this time with no regrets, because I didn't know when I would be back.

Tim gave me a hug and told us he had to hurry home and get some sleep before another early morning at the shop sneaked up on him. We took a silly photo on the top of the stairs, and as Cheri and I held up the rock 'n' roll sign with our hands, Tim made an odd sign with his. His two crossed fingers made us roar with laughter, and I couldn't think of a better note to end the night on. Oh, Tim!

Cheri, Jane and I shared one last fake beer before we decided to call it a night, too. When we exited out of the bar and onto Sunset Boulevard, Cheri told me she would walk ahead to her house so that Jane and I could have a moment. I nodded and told her I would meet her there after I got Jane into a car.

I grabbed Jane's hand as we crossed the street over to the gas station to wait for her Uber to arrive. It was an emotional moment. It was as if we had almost made up for all the lost time in those few short days, but there was still so much left to do. I wanted to stay there to support her in the sober endeavor she was undertaking. But, I knew I had to go.

"I really wish you could stay, Kaleb. I hope I can continue to be strong and stick to this lifestyle without you around," she said, as a few tears started to fall down her cheeks.

"I will be right here," I said, putting my hand over her heart. "And I will be right here, too," I reassured her, holding my phone up and shaking it a little.

"I'm gonna miss you so much, Kaleb. Text me every day!" she spoke, as she grabbed me for a really tight hug.

"I will. You got this, hunny. You are an amazingly strong woman. I'll be back before you know it. Love you."

A black Town Car pulled up as we hugged for the thousandth time, and it was hard to let her go. I hoped she would find the beauty of life through sobriety the way I had. She deserved it.

I closed the door and let a tear fall down my cheek as the car drove away. Okay, one down, one to go. I wiped my face with the sleeve of my jacket and headed over to Cheri's house a block away. I prepared myself for another emotional goodbye. This time I owed her an apology for leaving without saying a proper one before.

I knocked on her door and walked in with a full heart. "Well, this is it. Back to New York! I can't believe my trip is over already," I said, looking into my lovely British friend's loving brown eyes.

"I know! I'm really going to miss you. But I want you to know, you don't have to stay in an Airbnb the next time you come. You can always come stay with me anytime, love."

And with those last few words, I felt redeemed, justified and worthy. I know she wasn't in a position to give me a place to stay the last time I was about to leave Los Angeles, but this time, everything was different. We were both different, better, versions of our true selves. I smiled and without saying a word, leaped forward and gave her a huge hug. I had been waiting a long time for someone from my old life to truly see the new me and open up to me in a more stable, mature way. Our friendship grew even more that night, and I am grateful.

"Promise me it won't be over two years before we see you again! I love you, wifey," she said, holding my hand at her front door.

"I promise. Love you too, hubby," I replied, pulling her in for one last bear hug.

As I walked back down the street towards the Airbnb apartment, I took in the sights of the Sunset Strip one last time. I couldn't help but grin as I strolled in the glow of the city lights. What an emotional, fulfilling trip it had been! It couldn't possibly get any more amazing, could it? Oh, yes it could. Turns out there were a few more magical surprises awaiting me the next day, my final morning in LA.

THURSDAY.
DAY NINE.

THIS IS IT. Last day in Hollywood. Seemed like there were still some things I wanted to do. I was still mentally kicking myself for not actually speaking to Liam when I had the chance. I didn't get to actually say those words I had written to him in the last chapter of my book. I didn't get to tell him, "Thank you for breaking my heart. It helped save my life." I don't know why I had frozen when I saw him, but maybe it was because I had built the moment up so much in my head that whatever happened wouldn't have been "right." Not that life works that way, anyway. There wasn't always a storybook ending to every relationship or adventure, and I guess this was just how that chapter of my life with him was supposed to end. An open ending, really. Maybe I would get to say those words to him one day, but it wouldn't be today.

So, as I accepted that outcome as final, I headed out to the patio for my morning routine. Still in my NYU sweat pants and t-shirt, I pressed my finger down on my iPhone to open the mail app. The first letter I opened revealed a very welcomed surprise. It was a note from the president of Readers' Favorite congratulating me on winning a medal in their 2016 awards! Wow! Talk about a nice way to start the day.

I tried to hold back a tear, sitting on that wooden bench overlooking the sunlit street of West Hollywood, but it was no use. It fell anyway. This was another beautiful moment in my life that I almost couldn't believe was happening. It was the confirmation I needed to prove that my words did, in fact, have power and that the message in my book was affecting people in a positive way.

I had felt similar emotions and gratitude when I received my first 5-star review from them, but this, this was different; this was big. I had beat out so many other talented and worthy nonfiction writers to receive the award, a feat I had hoped for, but never quite put much faith into. I mean, I always had faith in my words, my story, and its message, but it being my first book, I was nervous about how my writing style would be accepted.

And this news meant that I was now an award-winning author. A title that if you had asked me two and a half years before would happen, sitting in the basement TV room at the Melrose Homeless Shelter, I would have laughed. Back then, finding ways to get enough money for my next drink, or wondering where my next hot meal would come from, were the only things on my mind. I said a silent prayer of thanks for the continued blessings and light that the Universe had bestowed upon me.

I quickly wrote a Facebook post sharing the news and the response was overwhelming. Messages of congratulations and love poured in almost immediately, and the kind words and support flowed in throughout the day. It was almost unbelievable to think that the magical week I had just experienced was real and that it was coming to an end already. I hurried back into my room, performed my daily face routine, got dressed, and packed my suitcase full of clothes and new memories. One of those memories was a picture of Justin Bieber holding my book that Tim had printed out for me the day before.

I said my goodbyes to Mimi and Diana in another heartfelt moment. I had not known them for long, but they had been so kind and were there every night to hear about one of the craziest, most beautiful, weeks of my life. They became great friends to me, and I was gonna miss seeing them every day. "I am beyond proud of you. Anytime you come back to LA, you are welcomed to stay with us," said Mimi, holding out her arms for one last hug.

"Thank you, ladies. Thank you," I said with a smile, as I slid my black sunglasses onto my face.

The next and last stop was the cake shop. Tim worked out his schedule so he would be free to take me to the airport. There were a few more sweet goodbyes at the bakery, but I didn't get overly emotional because I knew I would be back before too long. I was no longer afraid of what might happen in Los Angeles. In fact, I was looking forward to the next opportunity that allowed me to return.

Tim pulled his silver SUV in front of the shop and with my trusty messenger bag draped across my chest, I wheeled my big suitcase out to the sidewalk. I waved goodbye to the staff and felt a sense of relief as I opened the vehicle door. I had come to LA and accomplished more than I had ever expected. I had been so nervous and so scared of all the "what could be," that I seriously had considered cancelling at the last minute. I was thankful that I didn't let that frightened dark voice win.

We drove down La Cienega, and when we passed a certain building, I had a flashback from the very first week I came to LA. It was Bobby Trendy's old store. I was a huge fan of The Anna Nicole Show back in the day, and when I came to Hollywood, I knew I had to meet the lovable character I had seen on the show. I met him; we became friends, and I even went with him to a big celebrity's house to drop off some luxury pillows. That's when I was dating a porn star, too. But I think I'll save those stories for another time, maybe another book.

Tim pointed out to me that we were coming up on the Hilton LAX, and I quickly got out my phone to take a picture. It was there that the sad, desperate, broken down version of me spent my last night in Los Angeles two and a half years before. It was uplifting to pass by it now, after growing so much as a person. I don't think I would even recognize the person I was that night. He was gone and, God willing, he was never coming back.

We pulled up to the departure terminal, and I started to get emotional again. Tim was quick to speak. "I am so unbelievably proud of you. This is the person I love to see, the person I enjoy talking to on the phone, the person I know can do anything he puts his mind to. You have accomplished so much in such a relatively short amount of time. I can't wait to see what you do next!"

"Thank you. You know you mean the world to me. You know you're like the father I never had. I truly appreciate everything you do. Thanks for believing in me. Hopefully, I'll see you in a few months. Just gotta go rule the world first. Haha," I said, making a joke so that a tear wouldn't creep out of my eyes.

He opened the back of his car, and I removed my suitcase. He drove off as I started to walk in, and I was missing him and all my LA friends already. I hadn't even left yet! It had been such an amazing trip. I didn't want it to end! Fortunately, the magic that had surrounded the trip thus far was not done with me yet.

After checking in and quickly passing through the priority TSA line, I decided to grab a bite to eat before heading over to my designated Virgin America gate. I wrote my farewell Facebook post, and as I was in the middle of submitting it, I got a notification. Someone had tagged me in an article that the UK's Daily Mail had posted. The headline read: *"Fan buys Justin Bieber's lunch when his credit card is declined."*

The story went on to say that a nameless "Belieber" stepped in to pay for his meal in the embarrassing situation. Wait?! So, someone sold the story? I continued reading, and it stated that an employee at Subway had in fact leaked the news. Well, I was hoping that the story wouldn't get out, but first off, I wouldn't consider myself a "Belieber." I mean, I like his work, but I don't have all his records or go to concerts or impersonate him or anything. And really, there was a better story there that the writers of the article totally missed.

Then the posts kept coming. Same story, but in different languages and on many different websites. I saw that Us Weekly had mentioned it on their site, so I decided to tell my side of the story in the comments section. I didn't have much time to write something in depth because my departure time was closing in. I simply commented that I was the one who paid for it and that he had been extremely gracious for the gesture. I also mentioned that he gladly accepted a copy of my memoir, and I hoped he would be inspired by it if he read it.

I received a few comments from random people in response. Most of them were very kind and said that I did a really nice thing, a random act of kindness. Other people said some nasty things about me and him. I didn't exactly have time to answer everything at the moment, so I decided to wait until I got back to NYC to worry about it.

It was kind of funny, thinking my story had made world press, but the words that were being written didn't really explain what was actually going on in that moment. There was something much bigger than a "fan" buying his lunch, and I hoped I would figure out a way to tell what really happened, now that the story had been leaked. I giggled at the thought that I now had to "come forward" as the guy who bought one of the biggest stars in the world his lunch.

In my aisle seat on the jumbo jet, I opened up the note app on my phone and began to write the story how I thought it should have been told. I figured when I got back to my apartment in the city, I would then post it to my website and maybe add it to the comment sections of all the different publications that were reporting the news. I wrote a one-page piece and then relaxed in my chair to watch a movie.

The plane ride was over before I knew it, and we had landed. The flight attendants reminded everyone to check their seat back pockets for anything they might have left. So, I did. And what I found really shook me to the core.

Resting in the bottom of the fabric fold, I felt a piece of cardboard that resembled an envelope. I dug it out and found out it was a necklace in a clear plastic covered package. But this was not just any necklace, it was a Saint. A sterling silver coin with the engraving of Saint Anthony holding a little boy. It looked like something maybe a nun would give out, or something you might buy at a church gift shop. Like it had been left there on purpose for someone to find. I took it as a sign from above that the piece of jewelry was meant for me and placed it in my bag. I would have to do a little research on the Uber ride home to find out what this Saint was all about.

Baggage claim was a breeze, and the car arrived within minutes, my home address already appearing in the driver's GPS. I slid in to the backseat and pulled the necklace package out of my messenger bag. When I opened it up I found the prayer that was inscribed inside the card. It all made sense after I read the words:

"O Holy Saint Anthony, gentlest of Saints, your love for God and charity for His creatures, made you worthy to possess miraculous powers. Miracles wait on your word, which you are ever ready to speak for those in trouble or anxiety."

I'm no Saint, but the words kind of fit perfectly to the new life I was trying to lead. I wanted my words to be the power that helped others in trouble or those dealing with anxiety. And believe me, I loved the Creator more than I could ever explain. How could I not? He had blessed me beyond words, and every day I remembered to be grateful. And charity was something I tried to do all the time. Not just paying for a celebrity's meal, but doing what I could for anybody I met who needed a hand when I was able to give.

This necklace was like the Powers That Be telling me, "You have found your path. Continue on it, and your blessings will become blessings for others. Be a light, and then share it with everyone you meet. I am by your side."

Talk about a storybook ending. A magical ending to a trip I thought I might never take, a trip I would never have been able to take had I not gotten sober in that shelter. It's funny how the world works. How your plans are never really YOUR plans. That something greater than we are has made up its mind on how we should live, and when we find that perfect path, the blessings come without our asking. It isn't easy to find the path, but when you find it, you know.

Back in the Bronx, I wheeled my luggage into my beautiful apartment and threw myself down on my black leather couch. I let out the biggest sigh I think I had ever released. What a week! Before I headed to bed, I uploaded the story I had written on the plane to my website with a couple of the paparazzi pictures included. I replied to a few of the comments I had received on the Us Weekly post and added my response to a few of the other websites that were sharing the "unnamed fan" news.

I didn't know what to expect from all this talk about what happened, but I just hoped that somehow it would inspire people in the end. I had no clue what was about to happen next. The Creator had some big plans brewing, some extra magic to perform. Let's just say that I was completely surprised and humbled by the events that would take place my first few weeks back in New York.

EPILOGUE.
ONE WEEK BACK IN NYC.

FRIDAY was my first full day back in New York, but I stayed at home and spent the day submitting for acting work and responding to the various posts on which I had posted my story. I was kind of shocked that no one from these big publications had reached out to me for an exclusive interview yet. Even Bette Midler had made a joke on her Facebook page about the news! I felt hopeless that I would ever get my side of the story out there in a big way and that the whole story might blow over before I was able to really shed some light on the situation. Lacy's mom had other plans though.

Lacy's mother, Nancy, had always been a big supporter and fan of mine. We had a lovely online relationship, and she was always like an "online mom" to me. Makes sense because her daughter and I considered each other like brother and sister. On this day, she messaged me and asked, *"Would it be okay if I tell one of the local radio station hosts about your story? I bet they would love to interview you!"*

I agreed and figured it might be cool to do a radio interview, and that way I could at least get the word out there about how grateful he had been and that he had taken a copy of my book. She told me she would work on it and that she would get back to me soon.

About an hour went by, and she messaged me again. *"Okay, so this female DJ I listen to every day, KJ on 107.9, said she wants to speak to you, so I gave her your number. Looking forward to hearing you on Indy Radio!"*

And within the hour, the radio host called me. We had a great conversation, and I told her all about the crazy moments surrounding the good deed. She also asked me about my book, and I felt confident that at least the people of Indiana would hear my story! It wasn't world press, but it was my first radio interview, and it was fabulous.

There were some comments coming in to the post I had made on the Us Weekly site that were not so positive, though. People saying, "Oh, you're just trying to sell your book." Or, "You just bought him lunch 'cause he is a star." I was kinda shocked that people would respond in that way about a genuine good deed. So, I replied to a few of them and decided to take it one step further.

Amazon allows authors to run a week-long promotion where they can give their eBook away for free. I immediately put that into effect and posted the link to all the comments sections I had been writing in. My point for trying to get my story out there was not for world-wide fame; it was to get the message of hope that lay within my book out into the eyes of the people. I started to see the book being downloaded in record numbers after every link I posted. That made me happy because I knew that my book might be the thing that one of those people who would read it really needed to make a positive change in their life.

I turned off all my devices a little later in the evening and just had to take a step away from it all for a moment. It was sensational that so many people were taking an interest in my story, but it still wasn't what I had hoped it would be. One hundred or so individual responses and a radio interview were great, but I wanted to get the message out there in a bigger way. So, in bed that night, in my apartment in the Bronx, I said an extra prayer for a sign leading me to what I was supposed to do next. And maybe, for a little help along the way.

Saturday, finally back in Manhattan, I returned to work at Parigot. Catherine was excited to hear about all of the magic that had occurred in LA. She was so genuinely happy for me, and it was so wonderful to have a motherly figure in my real life who cared so much to see me finally being successful and fulfilled.

Work was a breeze, and it was a relatively busy lunch shift. A regular customer of mine was there, and I told him about my encounter with Bieber. He just happened to work for the New York Times, and I figured he would be a good person to ask about how best to get my side of the story out there. The first question he asked was, "What's your angle? Why would a news outlet want to print your version of a story that is already out there?"

That made me think. What more would I have to offer by coming forward as the person who bought his lunch? Did I want the publicity? Sure, I did. But I wanted it so that people could find out about my book and hopefully those that needed to read the words in it, to get some inspiration or help, would find them. I wanted people who had been in a situation like mine, been addicted, been in a shelter... oh! There it is. There was my "angle."

"I was in a homeless shelter a year and a half ago, and now I'm an award-winning published author buying one of the biggest celebrities in the world his food when his credit card got declined! That has to be an inspiring angle if I ever heard one!" I said, not believing I hadn't thought of it before.

"Okay. Now, you've got something. I'm not sure the Times would write about it, but I do know someone who works at Page Six over at the New York Post. Let me send him this story and your contact info. No promises, but let's see what happens."

I poured my regular customer another glass of his favorite wine and picked up the tab myself. He might possibly have just given me the best gift I could have asked for. And if the story did come out, he would be giving me a platform to reach all the people I wanted to help. So, I crossed my fingers and hoped for the best.

Before my shift ended, the mailman dropped off some letters and a package. I stopped short of screaming when I looked at the large brown envelope and saw my name and where it had come from. The package was from The Supreme Court of The United States of America, Chambers of Justice Sotomayor.

What? Whoa!

Okay, let me back it up just a bit and tell you why I might have been receiving a package from the office of this amazing woman.

A few weeks before I went on my magical journey back to LA, I was serving another lunch shift at Parigot when I got a call from the Secret Service letting us know that a special guest would be dining there that afternoon. They hadn't told me who to expect, and at the time the elections were in full swing, so I figured it might be Clinton or even Trump. I hadn't expected it to be Justice Sotomayor, but I am so glad it was. I didn't know it, but we actually had a lot in common.

She came in that afternoon with a few of her family members and the Secret Service in tow. I sat them in a corner booth and helped them like I would any normal customers. I drew pictures with the young girl and talked openly and friendly with the Justice and the other adults. Apparently, Sotomayor was a fan of Parigot and had been there a few times in the past.

We had lovely conversations when I would come

to the table to check on them. She told me that she had grown up in the Projects in the Bronx and that she had fought her way out of poverty to make it to one of the highest offices in the Nation. Talk about an inspiration! I told her a little about my story and that I had lived in a shelter right next to the Projects. We bonded over common hardships and the success we had both been able to achieve despite adversity. And when their lunch was finished, they had nothing but praise for the food and service.

As I readied their bill, I grabbed a copy of my book and headed to the table. I sat next to the Supreme Court Justice and looked her in the eyes when I handed her my book and said, "I just want to personally thank you for being one of the judges who voted to approve national marriage equality. You don't know how much that means to me and my friends. I may not have found someone I want to marry yet, but because of you that is now a real option, and I am forever grateful. America is thankful for your service. If you don't mind, I'd love to give you a copy of my book."

She took me by the hand and said, "You are very welcome. Will you sign it for me?"

Wow. What an honor. So, I signed the book for her, reiterating the message I had just spoken and smiled as I helped them get ready to leave. When she got to the door she turned around and said, "You know, I'm going to read your book and if I make it back to the city sometime soon, I'll bring you a copy of my memoir! Nice meeting you. Keep doing exactly what you are doing. You are doing great."

It was a pretty beautiful sentiment to be left with, from one of the most powerful women in the country, but I knew she was very busy, so I never really expected to see her back at the restaurant with a copy of her book for me any time soon.

Turns out she wouldn't be back, but she was a lady of her word and that's exactly what was in the package that arrived that afternoon; a copy of her inspirational book, My Beloved World.

To say I was surprised would be an understatement. I was overwhelmed by the gift and felt so honored that she took the time to send it to me, but it was what was inside that made me tear up.

On the title page she wrote:

"Kaleb Christiansen, I admire your courage. -Sonia"

I just stood there for a second in awe. One of the Supreme Court Justices of The United States of America had actually taken the time to read my book and felt inspired to send me a copy of hers with that beautiful message. The magic in the air must not have dissipated yet. And I was floating again.

A few hours later, when the initial shock of that amazing gift wore off, I was getting ready to meet up with one of my New York City besties, Kayla, for her birthday party when I got a call from the reporter at the Post. He said he was definitely interested in my story and asked if I had an exclusive with any other news agencies.

When I told him no, he asked me to send him some pictures and more information, and he would see what he could do. We spoke a few more times before I headed to the party, and I was hopeful that something good might come out of it.

I had a lovely evening sharing my stories with Kayla and her other friends. It was nice to be with her and feel somewhat normal again after a crazy/beautiful past week of adventure. She always knew how to keep me grounded while throwing in some encouragement, too. It was nice to have such an amazing friend like her and others all over the place. I felt like the luckiest person in the world.

The next day, I felt even luckier. I woke up to a text message with a link to a Page Six article about me!! Wow, they moved fast in the news world. But the title of that article was what really got me. It read:

"Justin Bieber's sandwich savior was homeless a year ago."

And this was what the article said:

The mystery fan who bought Justin Bieber lunch at Subway when the pop star's credit card was embarrassingly declined was living in a New York homeless shelter just a year ago, Page Six has learned. And the guy offered Bieber financial aid so the star wouldn't have to face paparazzi outside where his girlfriend waited in a car.

Bieber's credit card was declined at a Subway sandwich shop in West Hollywood, Calif., last week when it was reported an anonymous fan stepped in and saved his bacon. "[Justin] put his card into the machine and it was declined. He said, 'I have to run out and get another card.' I decided to pay it for him to spare him the second trip out into the crush of about 20 photographers," Kaleb Christiansen exclusively told us. *"I said, 'I got it.' And he asked if I was sure."* And unlike the singer's bratty reputation, *"He was so thankful."*

Christiansen — *an actor who's now on his feet also working as a waiter at Soho restaurant Parigot* — has spent time living in *"four or five homeless shelters,"* he says, due to drug and alcohol addiction while chasing an acting career. (He also says he was the *"No. 1 Britney Spears impersonator in the country"* before his life hit the skids.)

Meanwhile, little Bieber's Fresh Value Meal — *plus three milks and some cookies* — totaled around $16. Christiansen told us he was planning to keep it all a secret till his good deed leaked. *"I wasn't going to tell anyone out of respect for him ... I didn't want it to get out that he had his card declined,"* he said.

The former homeless man was in LA to sign copies of his memoir, *"Hollywood Heartbreak, New York Dreams."* *"I told him I was having a book signing and invited him,"* Christiansen told us of Bieber. *"I gave him a copy of my book and he said, 'I'm actually leaving town. I will definitely read this.' And he patted me on the shoulder and left.*

"He was totally cool with me and took an interest in my book. I was living in a New York City homeless shelter a year ago, and now I'm buying one of the biggest stars in the world lunch."

Sandwich Savior? Haha. I loved it. If I had to have a title, no better one to have than one that had the word savior in it. I was really grateful that the Post had written my story, and I immediately jumped out of bed and headed down to see if it had made it in the actual print version, as well. It did! And within a few hours, it had been reposted by all of the biggest news outlets in the world.

All day I kept getting messages from friends and random people saying they had seen the article published on different entertainment and news sites. It was translated to a ton of different languages! I received an especially huge glowing response from the people In Brazil! By Wednesday my free eBook had been downloaded over a thousand times.

I felt so amazing, knowing that people were getting to experience my book, and I was hopeful that they would be inspired. The magic that had been predicted in the cards came true, and it exceeded any expectations I had ever imagined. And to think, it all started one night in a homeless shelter in Queens, the moment I decided to put the drinks and the drugs down for good.

My story is not over yet, but it begins anew every day. I want to leave you with one last thing. It is a message I received in my inbox a week or so after all the press came out.

The message read:

"Hi Kaleb,

You probably don't know who I am, but we went to high school together, I graduated in 2000.

My middle son is 10, almost 11. He came to me a couple

weeks ago and told me he is gay. Of course, I told him it's no big deal.

I haven't asked him how he knows about you, but he pulled you up and showed me your book and pictures of you.

He told me, 'This guy named Kaleb is one of my heroes.'

That's you. I just thought you might like to know that."

This one message touched my heart and made me realize that we are all leaving an important legacy for the next generation. You never know who your words or actions could be reaching. I want the lesson I leave to be one of hope and inspiration. And I pray that it reaches your heart, too.

We are never too old, hopeless, stressed, addicted or too far down into a rock bottom that we can't find a way out. There is always hope and help if we are willing to search for it.

I couldn't be prouder of what I have been able to accomplish through sobriety and the gifts that have come with it when I decided to finally take a chance on myself. Thank you for joining me on this journey. I hope you have been inspired. I've said it a million times, and I'll keep saying it until everyone knows: you can truly do anything you put your mind to if you believe in yourself and ask for the help you need.

Until next time, my friends. Stay Strong and Dream Big.

one week in LA
two years later

Just six months after the story in *Hollywood Heartbreak | New York Dreams* I was on my way back to the city that had been like a self-made hell, but this time with a clear mind and a divine purpose.

The week ahead would turn out to be more magical than I ever expected.

"Lady Catherine" reads the messages in the tarot cards the day before my trip that promise magic and an encounter with an old friend. Chef Michel looks on in support.

(Above) The airport cupcake and my ticket back to LA. I was nervous and excited about the possibilities.

(Right) The Instagram post that Book Soup released to promote my big event. Just a week before Spike Lee was signing books there. I was in good literary company.

(Above) With "Cheri" before and after glamming up for my first night back in LA. Seeing her again was so beautiful and long awaited.

(Left) With the cake shop patriarch and my personal spiritually adoptive father figure, "Tim," at the cake shop. They say, "you can never go home again" but I went home and proved them wrong. Back at the cake shop felt like home.

(Above) Recreating a scene from my first book at Hot n' Juicy.

(Below) Seeing the Beverly Hills sign with clear eyes was a first for me, too.

(Above) On the pink carpet with "Cheri" at the grand opening party of the Helen Ficalora store in Beverly Hills. I declined the offers of free champagne and felt very proud.

(Below) Seeing my poster in the window of the most famous book shop in Hollywood was a surefire sign that I was on the right path. I almost couldn't believe it!

(Left) Outside the mod Airbnb where I met Mimi and Diana. Those two girls became more than just temporary roommates, they became friends for life.

(Right) Having a nonalcoholic beer at Saddle Ranch on Sunset where I saw old acquaintances who were shocked to see the healthy and sober new me.

(Left) Having a virgin mojito at The Abbey where I ran into my old bartender friend Nate. Some people ask me how I can go to bars and be around alcohol while sober? Every recovering addict is different. My approach is to look my enemy in the eye and laugh then carry on with my life. Just because I'm sober doesn't mean I have to give up my social interactions.

(Below) The Sunset Strip. It was my home away from home and at one point I lived in two businesses there.

A paparazzi shot that caught me and Justin Bieber in the Subway restaurant on Sunset Boulevard on my second day back in Hollywood. Magic was in the air!

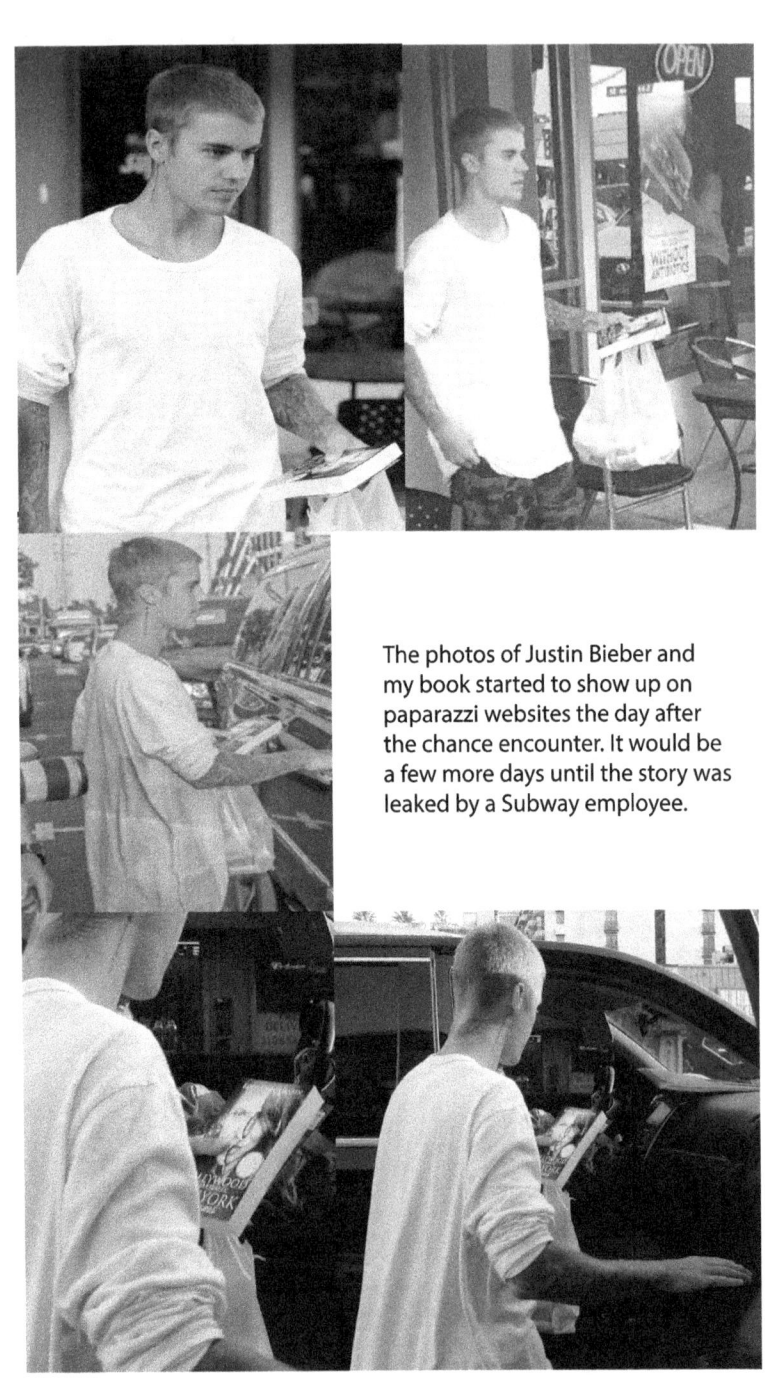

The photos of Justin Bieber and my book started to show up on paparazzi websites the day after the chance encounter. It would be a few more days until the story was leaked by a Subway employee.

(Left) With "Lacy" on the evening of the house party. When we saw each other again it was like no time had passed. Twin Power!

(Below) 10 years had passed since the first pic but one comment we received said we looked younger now,

The photos at the bottom of this page give you an inside look at "The State Room" and a sober-selfie shot taken in the bathroom where one of the most dramatic scenes in *Hollywood Heartbreak | New York Dreams* occurred.

My book signing event was one of my proudest moments. Being surrounded by old friends and people who truly cared about me was a wonderful feeling I hadn't felt since I was a child. It was a beautiful evening I will never forget.

(Above) The book signing after-party with "Lacy," "Tim," Cathy and her man, Michelle, Nikki and "Jane."

(Left) With my cigar mentor and dear friend Michelle.

(Below) "Cheri" snaps a pic of me on Joey's lap.

(Above) With Joey and a copy of my book at the after-party.

(Left) At Mel's Diner where Splenda on a table caused a big scene a few years before.

(Below) With a top hat very similar to the one I wore just about every night.

(Left) With "Lacy" at The Twisted Rainbow.

(Below) Having a heartfelt conversation with the lovely Kym.

Spending the day with "Jane" going back to all the old stomping grounds but this time sober and happy. It was a new experience for both of us. Tipping the dancer at the bar in West Hollywood made my day!

Monday with "Cheri" was my first sober trip over the hills of Hollywood to the WB Studio for the taping of the Conan O'Brien show. A beautiful day weather wise and emotionally.

 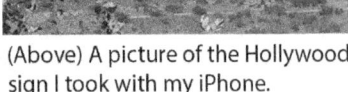

(Above) With the giant Conan bobble head statue at WB Studios.

(Above) A picture of the Hollywood sign I took with my iPhone.

Outside the studio waiting for our VIP cart to take us to set.

Flashback picture of me and David Beckham chillin' at Coffee Bean.

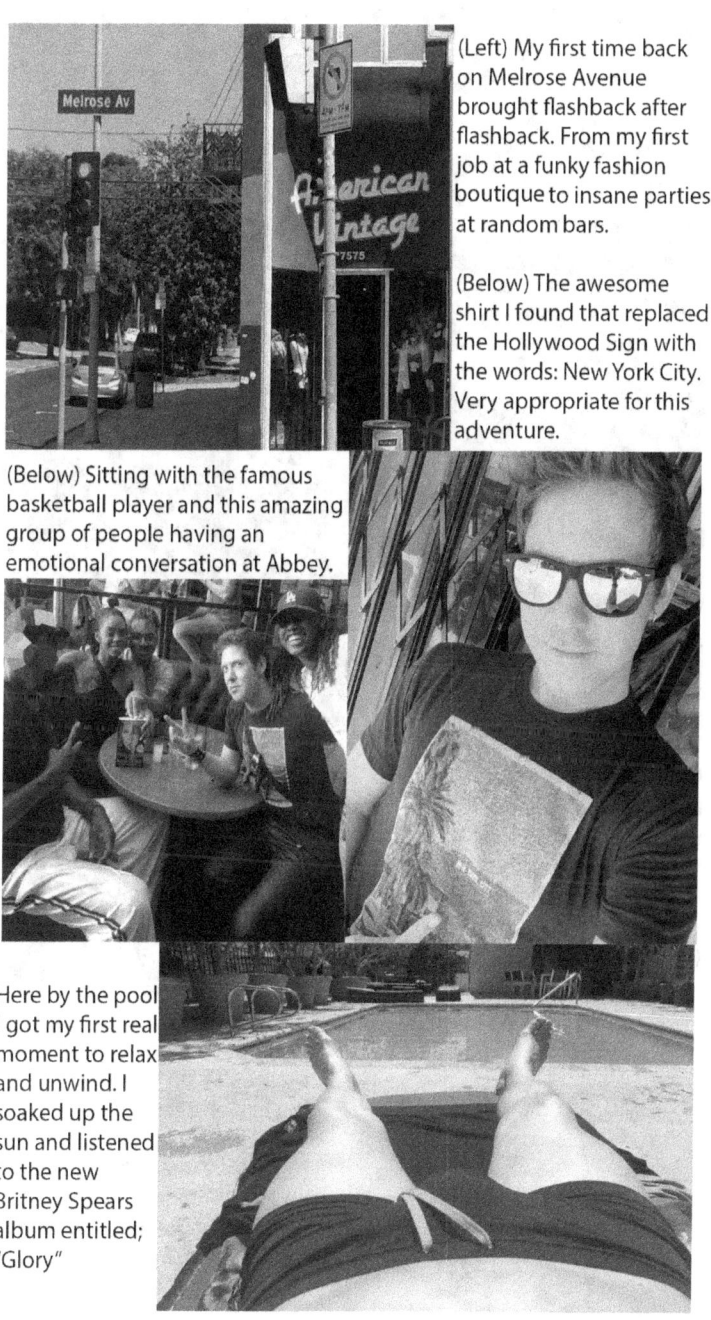

(Left) My first time back on Melrose Avenue brought flashback after flashback. From my first job at a funky fashion boutique to insane parties at random bars.

(Below) The awesome shirt I found that replaced the Hollywood Sign with the words: New York City. Very appropriate for this adventure.

(Below) Sitting with the famous basketball player and this amazing group of people having an emotional conversation at Abbey.

Here by the pool I got my first real moment to relax and unwind. I soaked up the sun and listened to the new Britney Spears album entitled; "Glory"

My second "final Wednesday in LA" and I was performing again at "The Twisted Rainbow." But this time I had dear friends to cheer me on. (Above) You can see "Jane" and "Tim" shooting video.

(Right) "Tim" flashing his rock 'n' roll crossed finger sign. Oh, "Tim!"

Getting the news that my book had won a medal in the Readers' Favorite Awards Contest, on my last morning in Hollywood, made for the perfect and most magical ending to my trip. But the magic wasn't through with me yet...

(Above) The last two things I saw before arriving at the airport for my flight back to NYC. Two years prior the Hilton LAX was the place I spent my last drunken evening before escaping to New York and eventually finding my true self again.

(Below) The prayer in the envelope holding the necklace that I found while on the plane. A sure sign from The Creator that I was on the right path.

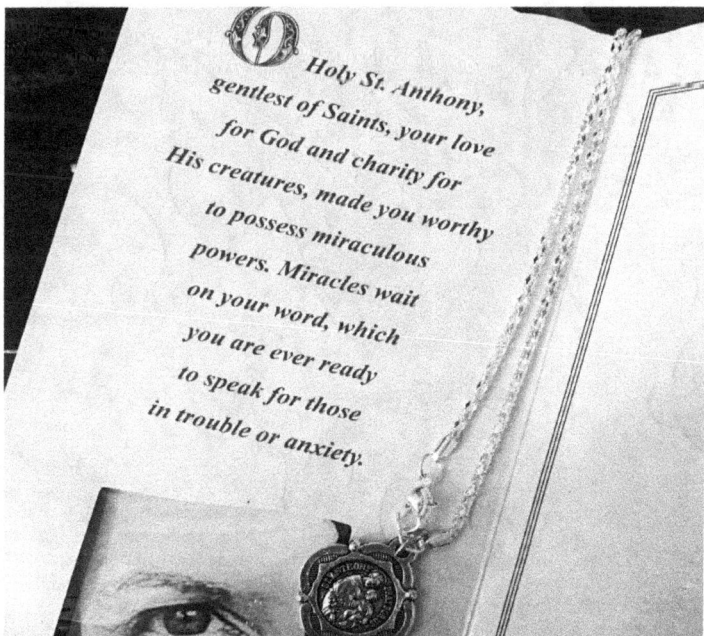

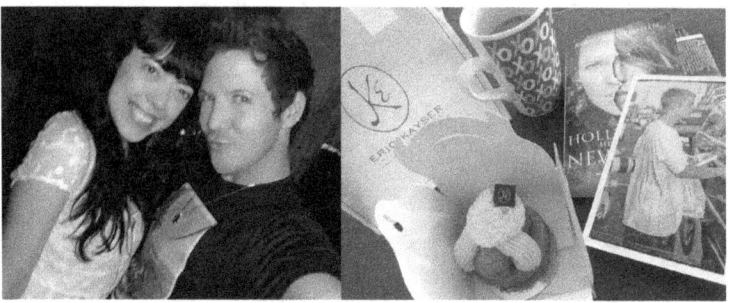

(Above) Back in NYC it was business as usual. Celebrating Kayla's birthday and a welcome home pastry from my coworker at Parigot. I didn't know it at the moment but the magic from my LA trip wasn't over yet.

I was shocked when this package arrived from the Supreme Court. I am so deeply honored that this amazing, brave, strong, resilient woman took the time to send me a signed copy of her memoir after reading mine. I will cherish this gift forever. Thank you, Justice Sotomayor for continuing to inspire me and millions of others.

Page Six of the New York Post ran a page-heading article about my encounter with Bieber.

BESTSELLERS: August 22 - 28

FICTION HARDCOVER

1. *The Girls* (Emma Cline)
2. *Woman in Cabin 10* (Ruth Ware)
3. *The Regulars* (Georgia Clark)
4. *Before the Fall* (Noah Hawley)
5. *Underground Railroad* (Colson Whitehead)
6. *Bright Precious Days* (Jay McInerney)
7. *Last Days of Night* (Graham Moore)
8. *Sweetbitter* (Stephanie Danler)
9. *Dark Matter* (Blake Crouch)
10. *The Gentleman* (Forrest Leo)

FICTION PAPERBACK

1. *The Goldfinch* (Donna Tartt)
2. *The Secret History* (Donna Tartt)
3. *Man From Atlantis* (Patrick Duffy)
4. *Vegetarian* (Han Kang)
5. *The Sympathizer* (Viet Thanh Nguyen)
6. *The Handmaid's Tale* (Margaret Atwood)

NON-FICTION HARDCOVER

1. *Art of Tough* (Barbara Boxer)
2. *2 Chairs* (Bob Beaudine)
3. *Tears to Triumph* (Marianne Williamson)
4. *Powerhouse* (James Andrew Miller)
5. *Altamont* (Joel Selvin)
6. *Chancers* (Susan Stellin)
7. *Building Art* (Paul Goldberger)
8. *Hillbilly Elegy* (J.D. Vance)
9. *The Girl With the Lower Back Tattoo* (Amy Schumer)
10. *Live Fast Die Hot* (Jenny Mollen)

NON-FICTION PAPERBACK

1. *Find a Way* (Diana Nyad)
2. *Hollywood Heartbreak, New York Dreams* (Kody Christiansen)
3. *M Train* (Patti Smith)
4. *Just Kids* (Patti Smith)
5. *Wonderland Avenue* (Danny Sugerman)

(Above) Proudly holding my copy of The New York Post in a park in the city. I hoped the story would bring the eyes of those who needed help to the words in my book. I didn't expect what happened next.

(Right) A few days after my book signing event Book Soup released their bestsellers list. I was thrilled to see my memoir at #2. Making the list of one of the most famous bookstores in Hollywood was a big deal.

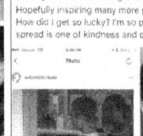

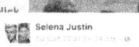

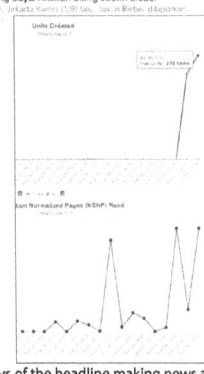

The inspiring story of a good deed made headline news around the world!

Within days of the headline making news and my choice to give my eBook away for free in conjunction, over a 1,000 people downloaded my book and it became #1 on Amazon. I was hopeful that people who might need to be inspired were amongst the downloaders.

Finally had my Elle Woods moment at Harvard when I signed books at the university. I had never really dreamed that my life would end up taking such a beautiful turn.

(Below) I was in headline celebrity gossip news once again but this time it was for my featured role in the new film: *Ocean's Eight*. Caught by paparazzi while shooting this scene on the streets of New York. Pictured with me are Cate Blanchett and Helena Bonham Carter. My old scene buddy, Sandra Bullock, was here, too.

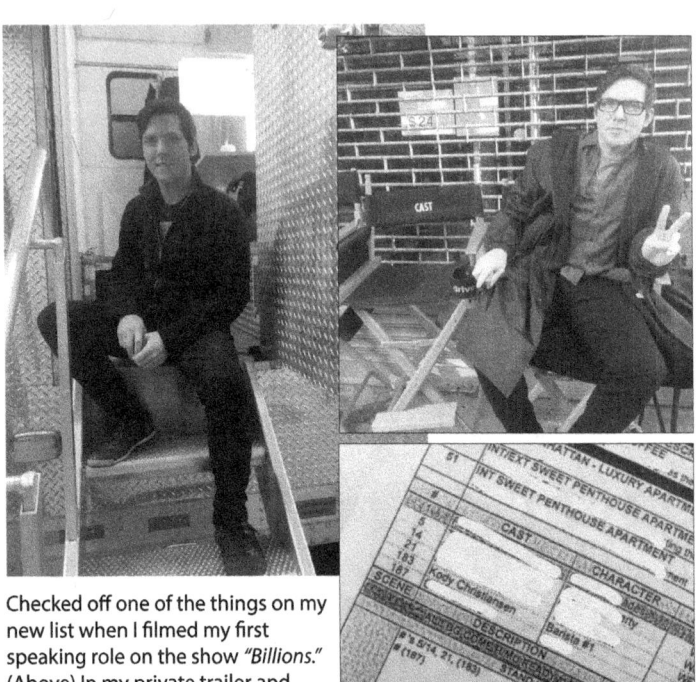

Checked off one of the things on my new list when I filmed my first speaking role on the show *"Billions."* (Above) In my private trailer and sitting in a cast chair. (Right) My name on the cast list. (Below) A screen shot from playback.

I saved the most important picture for last.

While all the memories the other photos hold are amazing and beautiful, it is this comparison photo that makes me the proudest. Seeing the transformation in myself over the last two years is the best gift I have gotten from sobriety. It is not just a physical change but the emotional and mental changes that happen when you take a chance on yourself and find your true path.
We can all share this common joy if we remember to STAY STRONG and DREAM BIG.

ACKNOWLEDGEMENTS

Keeping the name change

Although this is a true story I have continued the tradition of the name changes from the first book. This was done to protect the identities of certain people as well as give me the opportunity to write myself with a different name to sort of step back from the very real emotional issues discussed in the series. So, these are my roman a clef (a fun French word I learned for a book like mine) and I couldn't be more proud of how my words have inspired so many already.

Tom

Oh, Tom. My father figure. Thank you for granting me the ability to follow my dreams and always supporting my latest endeavors. I don't know where I'd be without you and I'm glad I won't ever have to find out. Love you.

Sarah K.

My darling friend Sarah, thank you for being the first set of eyes to see this work and offer your edits and advice. I am beyond proud of this book and I owe you a big thanks for the help. Thanks for loving our Chauncy for all these years. Xo

Ms. Edgintgon (Bettye!)

My high school English instructor and one of my all-time favorite teachers! So glad we reconnected after all these years. Thank you for offering to edit my second book. Working with you on this project has been like a crazy full circle moment. I hope you are proud of your student now. I think you did an amazing job. Enjoy retirement traveling the world. You deserve it!

My French Family

To Catherine and Michel. I can't believe our place is gone. I am so grateful for the time we shared there and the lessons I learned. I love you like family. And although the restaurant may be gone physically, it will remain forever in my heart and the hearts of all the customers who loved it and you, so much. Your blue-eyed son.

Ms. Pompay and The Organization

Ms. Pompay. Thank you for the amazing support over the last year and a half. I feel like I have known you forever. Thank you for always being proud of me. I wish you the best always. Love you. And to "The Organization" I give my utmost gratitude and respect. Without you and your services I wouldn't have been able to spread my wings so far or fly so high. Much love to you all. Keep helping those who need it. You are a true blessing to so many.

Book Soup, Harvard, McNally

A big thanks to three special bookstores.

Book Soup, thank you for hosting my Los Angeles book signing. This whole second book would not even exist had you not offered me the amazing opportunity to share my story that night in August at your store.

Harvard Bookstore, thank you for believing in me and offering me the chance to have my work seen by some of the brightest minds in the country. I look forward to my next trip to Cambridge! Spencer, you are awesome!!

And McNally Jackson. Jacob, thank you for all the hard work you have put into helping me make these books a reality. Your energy, support and belief in me has helped me to achieve more than I ever thought I could in such a short period of time. I'm forever thankful. And Margaret, you rock! Thanks for helping me make all the last-minute changes. I'm so glad you guys are my partners in publishing!

Readers' Favorite

To the President, Staff and every author I met at the Readers' Favorite Awards in Miami, thank you for the inspiration! Receiving my first book award on that stage, surrounded by talented writers, made me feel very special. I am so proud to have been honored in that way by such an amazing organization and even better group of people. Thank you!

Mimi and Diana

My girls!!! Thank you for my first Airbnb experience and for showing me the most amazing hospitality ever. Diana - I wish you nothing but the best in the future. Mimi - it was so amazing to have that full circle moment with you. I pray that you are blessed. Thanks for being a great friend and an awesome temporary roommate!

"Jane"

Wow! The years have flown by and I am so glad we are still in each other's lives. The world has sometimes been rough for us but we are two tough kitties and I'm happy we made it through it all. So unbelievably proud of you for taking the steps to enjoy a different side of life. May your light pass on to others daily. Love you more than words can express.. so I'll just say, "meow meow!"

Page Six

To Carlos and everyone at Page Six, thank you for taking on my story and helping me spread the message of perseverance and random acts of kindness to the world. Together we inspired lots of people with the printed word. I'm forever in your debt. Looking forward to the next time we can make worldwide headlines together!

Everyone in LA

To everyone who greeted me with open arms and respect, I give my thanks. You made me feel even more at home in the place I used to be scared to call home. Thank you for being forgiving and for giving the new me the space to shine.

My mom

Ulla, your voice is my guide through the ups and downs of this crazy/beautiful world. Thank you for always being there for me in spirit. I felt you that day on the set of 'The Blacklist' when I was working with one of our favorite actresses.

I pray I keep making you proud every day.

Special little boy

To that special young man who called me one of his heroes, thank you. Knowing that I have inspired you, in turn, inspires me to keep reaching for new goals. You are a hero of mine, too. Coming out at a young age can be very scary and I am so proud of you for showing an exceptional amount of bravery. You are going to do great things with your life! I know it. Keep being exactly who you are and the world will open up in ways you never imagined. Can't wait to hear all the exciting updates from your mom. Stay Strong! Dream Big! Xo

RESOURCES FOR HOPE AND HELP

Los Angeles Homeless Services

LAHSA's Emergency Response Team offers people in the City and County of Los Angeles experiencing homelessness:

1. Direct emergency services and transportation.

2. Referrals to shelter for homeless families, unaccompanied adults, and youth.

3. Outreach services.

LAHSA Hotline: (213) 225-6581
Hours of Operation:
Monday through Friday, 7:30 a.m. to 4:30 p.m.
https://www.lahsa.org/homeless-resources/get-help

Los Angeles LGBT Center

Since 1969 the Los Angeles LGBT Center has cared for, championed, and celebrated LGBT individuals and families in Los Angeles and beyond. Today the Center's nearly 600 employees provide services for more LGBT people than any other organization in the world, offering programs, services, and global advocacy that span four broad categories: Health, Social Services and Housing, Culture and Education, Leadership and Advocacy. Despite our size, scope, and determination to meet the growing demand for our services, we remain a lean, fiscally disciplined organization, earning a four-star Charity Navigator rating for six consecutive years. We are an unstoppable force in the fight against bigotry and the struggle to build a better world, a world in which LGBT people can be healthy, equal, and complete members of society.

1625 N. Schrader Boulevard

Los Angeles, CA 90028-6213

323-993-7400

https://lalgbtcenter.org/about-the-center/contact-us

The Trevor Project Hotline

Our trained counselors are here to support you 24/7. If you are a young person in crisis, feeling suicidal, or in need of a safe and judgment-free place to talk, call the Trevor Lifeline now at

866-488-7386.

http://www.thetrevorproject.org/

Los Angeles Regional Food Bank

Pantry distribution dates and times are subject to change. Please call the pantry to verify that this information is current. Most pantries serve according to geographical service area. Food pantry clients should bring photo identification with them to the pantry. The identification should show client's current residential address. Some pantries have an application process and ask clients for documents supporting income. However, all clients will be served the first time regardless of completion of application and service area.

https://www.lafoodbank.org/get-help/pantry-locator/

GLBT National Help Center

The GLBT National Help Center is a non-profit, tax-exempt organization that is dedicated to meeting the needs of the gay, lesbian, bisexual and transgender (GLBT) community and those questioning their sexual orientation and gender identity. We offer two national hotlines. The first is the GLBT National Hotline for people of all ages (youth & adult). The second is the GLBT National Youth Talkline, specifically for callers age 25 and younger. We help end the isolation that many people feel, by providing a safe environment on the phone or via the internet to discuss issues that people often can't talk about anywhere else.

http://www.glbtnearme.org/

Narcotics Anonymous

Narcotics Anonymous is a global, community-based organization with a multi-lingual and multicultural membership. NA was founded in 1953, and our membership growth was minimal during our initial twenty years as an organization. Since the publication of our Basic Text in 1983, the number of members and meetings has increased dramatically. Today, NA members hold nearly 67,000 meetings weekly in 139 countries. We offer recovery from the effects of addiction through working a twelve-step program, including regular attendance at group meetings. The group atmosphere provides help from peers and offers an ongoing support network for addicts who wish to pursue and maintain a drug-free lifestyle. Our name, Narcotics Anonymous, is not meant to imply a focus on any particular drug; NA's approach makes no distinction between drugs including alcohol. Membership is free, and we have no affiliation with any organizations outside of NA including governments, religions, law enforcement groups, or medical and psychiatric associations. Through all of our service efforts and our cooperation with others seeking to help addicts, we strive to reach a day when every addict in the world has an opportunity to experience our message of recovery in his or her own language and culture.

www.na.org

ALCOHOLICS ANONYMOUS

Alcoholics Anonymous is an international fellowship of men and women who have had a drinking problem. It is nonprofessional, self-supporting, multiracial, apolitical, and available almost everywhere. There are no age or education requirements. Membership is open to anyone who wants to do something about his or her drinking problem.

www.aa.org

FAMOUS LAST WORDS

A FEW WEEKS later, I did end up having my moment with Liam. Although it was nothing like I had hoped for and left a lot more to be said. Cheri was able to get the copy of the book I left for him in his hands one night in a private meeting at a hotel in West Hollywood. She told me the only reason she would ever agree to see him was to give him the book for me. She was a true friend. She called me to tell me what happened.

She said that when he saw it, he only had good things to say about it and that he was happy to see me doing well. She also had to avoid his half-drunken attempt at flirting and suggestions of getting back together with her. Seemed like some things might never change. She also asked for his phone number because she thought I might want to reach out to him for the closure I was seeking.

I jotted down the number and didn't do anything with it until a few days later. After my lunch shift one day, I consulted with Tim and Catherine and decided to make the call. Sitting on the bench in front of Parigot, I tried to gather my thoughts before pressing the call button. I hoped I could find the right words to speak to his soul, to let him know that he still had someone that had his health and best interests in mind. I pressed the button and waited nervously as it rang.

"Hello?"

"Hey, Liam. It's Kaleb..." I said. And before I could speak another word, he interrupted.

"Hey! Wow, it's so good to hear your voice. I got that copy of your book you left. You look really good on the cover. Healthy. Happy?" he said, turning the last compliment into a question.

"Yeah. I am happy. I've been sober for over a year, and my life has never been better," I replied, still waiting for the right moment to tell him exactly what I had been waiting two and half years to say.

"That's great. I'm really happy for you, and I'm gonna read your book. I just need to find some time alone, where no one bothers me. You know my ADD acts up sometimes. But, hey! I just got to the Rainbow for lunch. I really need to eat something, it's been like three days since I had my last real meal. Can I call you back later?"

"Sure, Liam. Sure. Just make sure you read the pages I wrote about in my note," I said, almost knowing that I wouldn't hear from him again that day. And I was right. I didn't. I didn't hear from him again after that, and when I tried to call him again a week later, his phone had been disconnected (or he lost it in a blackout and got yet another burner phone). I didn't know if I would ever speak to him again, but I did have plans to return to Hollywood the next year, so anything could happen.

Speaking of plans! A lot of the list that I spoke about in chapter 4 has already been completed by the time I finished writing this book. In the months after my visit to LA, I had a book signing at Harvard. The trip to Boston with my bestie, Kayla, was one I will never forget. I finally had my Elle Woods moment on the steps of Harvard Law School, light years away from the homeless shelter where my journey had begun.

And weeks after that, I had my second ever big television audition for a role on the huge Showtime series, *Billions*, and I got the part! I portrayed a hipster barista and had my first lines. I had my first private trailer and signed a contract to be billed as a co-star in the credits when the show aired. I was proud to share my first ever speaking role scene with a gender non-conforming actor named Asia Kate Dillion who is becoming a pioneer for the LGBTQ community with this groundbreaking role. We connected, and I passed on a copy of my book.

I also travelled to Miami to collect my Readers' Favorite Award on another amazing trip with Kayla. The fellowship of talented authors and fascinating new friends I made inspired me to keep writing the tales of my adventures in hopes to inspire more people.

And finally, I set up a book signing in my hometown of Fort Worth, Texas, to happen two days before Christmas Eve. The event was scheduled to take place at the bookstore where I had spent many hours with my mother and friends as a child. I thought that would definitely make for a beautiful full circle moment. l was nervous, just thinking about seeing all the people from my past; my friends, my exes and mostly, my family. But this year was all about facing my fears, making amends, redemption and inspiration. It was a trip that I had to take.

I would finally be home for the holidays, thirteen years later.

www.ingramcontent.com/pod-product-compliance
Lightning Source LLC
Chambersburg PA
CBHW071613080526
44588CB00010B/1111